THE REAL MR. BIG

HOW A COLOMBIAN REFUGEE BECAME THE UNITED KINGDOM'S MOST NOTORIOUS COCAINE KINGPIN

RON CHEPESIUK
JESUS RUIZ HENAO

WILD BLUE
PRESS

WildBluePress.com

THE REAL MR. BIG published by:
WILDBLUE PRESS
P.O. Box 102440
Denver, Colorado 80250

WILDBLUE PRESS is registered at the U.S. Patent and Trademark Offices.

ISBN 978-1-952225-58-1 Trade Paperback
ISBN 978-1-952225-57-4 eBook

Cover design © 2021 WildBlue Press. All rights reserved.

Interior Formatting/Book Cover Design by Elijah Toten
www.totencreative.com

THE REAL MR. BIG

Table of Contents

"Fortune Sides With Him Who Dares."
* Virgil
Ancient Roman poet of the Augustan Age

"We are looking at the first billion-pound drug cartel we have ever dealt with."
* Mark Malloy
Detective Superintendent of the United Kingdom National Crime Squad

FOREWORD

The genesis for this book came in May 2017 from an email sent from the United Kingdom. The letter writer was the daughter of Jesus Ruiz Henao, and she explained to me that her father had asked her to write to me. He wanted to know if I would be interested in writing a book about him. She noted that I had mentioned him in my book *Drug Lords,* a history of Colombia's Cali Cartel.

The daughter provided some details about her father. He was serving time in a British prison, but would be out by July 2017. She provided some links to internet articles about her father. At this stage, I knew nothing about Jesus, but the links intrigued me. Grabbing my attention in reading the articles was the claim that Jesus was one of the first billion-pound drug dealers in United Kingdom history.

The articles told about how he had emigrated to the United Kingdom and quietly ran his drug-trafficking network under the noses of British authorities for several years. In one of the articles, MI5, Great Britain's security agency, claimed that the price of cocaine had increased by fifty percent after his takedown.

The more I read, the more excited I got. I didn't think I would write another book. I had turned the focus of my writing career towards screenwriting, and I told friends that it would take a special project to deflect me from my goal of seeing one of my scripts on the big screen. I wrote the daughter back, telling her I would be interested in collaborating on her father's story. She arranged to have her father call me from the UK where he was incarcerated.

The conversation went well, and we agreed that we would collaborate on his life story once he was freed from prison. We were hoping it would be July, but his release date kept getting pushed back because of some legal wranglings. Time marched on, and I was beginning to have my doubts that he would be released. But finally in mid-2019, I got word from his daughter that her father was going to be released shortly. That happened on 10 October 2019, and Jesus was immediately deported to Colombia I gave Jesus time to settle in, and then we discussed signing a contract for the project. Once we got that done, we agreed on a time when I would travel to Colombia to interview him and collect some materials he had on his life and criminal career.

I arrived in Bogotá in late January 2020, just as the coronavirus was about to change the world. I spent several days with Jesus, taping his amazing story. I returned home and put together a book proposal. WildBlue Press agreed to publish the book.

What follows is one of the unique stories in the history of the War on Drugs. This is the story of an ambitious Colombian refugee who migrated to the United Kingdom and set up a sophisticated drug trafficking organization. It is a story that earned Jesus Ruiz Henao the infamous title, as British law enforcement described him, of being "the Pablo Escobar of British drug trafficking."

PROLOGUE

THE RAID

27 November 2003
91 Herndon Way, London, United Kingdom

Jesus Ruiz Henao: "I knew they would come for me, but I did not think it would be at four o'clock in the morning in front of my wife and kids. I had another restless night. I awoke, naked, and had made my way to the bathroom. I could hear the movement in the street down below, doors opening and closing, men getting out of the vehicles, mumbles that sounded like orders. I looked through the window, and my heart pounded. It was a police raid.

"I hurried to my desk in the bedroom and grabbed a piece of paper with my most important phone numbers. I barely had time to swallow the paper before the police barged through the front door and fanned out through the house, shouting: 'Police, police!' Two of the officers, guns drawn, dashed up the stairs and were at the bedroom door.

"'Christ, look at this,' one of them, the tall police officer, said as he peered into the bathroom and gawked at my naked form. The second officer flashed his warrant card and introduced himself. He asked: 'Are you Jesus Ruiz Henao?' I nodded yes. He then said: 'You are under arrest for conspiracy to supply a controlled drug, namely cocaine, and conspiracy to launder the proceeds of money laundering. I advise you that anything you say from this point could be used against you in a court of law.' I was stunned and did not reply.

"They gave me some clothes from the bedroom, and I got dressed. I could hear my wife, Maria, and children crying. I wanted to comfort them, but the tall officer advised me to let them be. For some reason, he asked if I spoke English. I said: 'Yes.' Then I was asked if I could read and write English and again I replied: 'Yes.'

"Back downstairs, they put handcuffs on me and sat me down on the sofa. My wife was brought into the living room, shivering. With a look of despair, she mumbled: 'What is going on, Jesus?' I tried to reassure her, but I could tell she didn't believe me. I was pissed. They had arrested me in front of my family. They didn't have to do it in my house. They had plenty of chances to do it in the street. They had been following me for months.

"I watched as one of the officers took video footage of each room. Computer equipment, mobile phones, and a digital satellite receiver were put carefully in plastic bags and carted away. A policeman grabbed a hundred-year-old bottle of scotch I had stored in the liquor cabinet for special occasions, opened it, and took a swallow. He looked at me and licked his lips. The arrogant bastard smiled.

"Finally, I was told to stand, and I was escorted to an unmarked police car. I watched as my wife was put in another car. I was told I was going to Charring Cross Police Station where I would be interviewed.

"We drove through the streets in silence, watching the Londoners hustle off to work. I thought about my own 'work,' which I had pursued in earnest, becoming what MI5 would later describe as the United Kingdom's first billion-pound cocaine dealer. I had been so careful for ten years, hiding my identity, making sure of the people with whom I dealt.

"Even now I was smug in my belief that I would never be caught. I was out of the drug trade. What could they possibly do to me?"

ONE

BEGINNINGS

Jesus Ruiz Henao is a leap year baby, born February 29, 1960, on a farm near Trujillo, a small town located in Colombia's Department of Valle del Cauca in southwest Colombia. Along Valle de Cauca's Pacific Ocean coastline are pristine beaches, while inland are the majestic Andes Mountains. The capital city Santiago de Cali is renowned as a center for salsa dancing and music, and for being the home base of the drug trafficking organization, the defunct Cali Cartel. Buenaventura is one of Colombia's busiest ports and has been a major conduit for drug trafficking.

Life was hard for Jesus and his family, but he had a happy childhood. He was the fifth eldest child of ten children (seven brothers and three sisters). His mother, Maria Henao de Ruiz, married his father, Jose Ruiz Betancourt, when she was just eighteen. She was a short woman with white skin, very loyal, and a hard worker, doing all the housework from 5 a.m. to 8 p.m. nearly every day. His father married his mother at the age of forty-two. He had dark skin and was a hard worker as well, toiling every day at the farm doing many different tasks.

Trujillo is seemingly quiet and sleepy, but it has an infamous history of terror. The town is infamous in Colombia for the horrible massacre dubbed the Massacre of Trujillo, a series of grisly murders in and around the town of three hundred and fifty to five hundred progressives, unionists, and farmers suspected of being ELN (National Liberation Army) guerilla supporters.

The National Liberation Army (ELN), Colombia's largest leftist guerrilla group, was formed in 1964 by brothers Fabio and Manuel Vásquez Castaño following the decade of the Colombian Civil War from 1948 to 1958, known as *La Violencia*. A Marxist-Leninist group, the ELN sought to defend Colombians who it believed to be victims of social, political, and economic injustices perpetrated by the Colombian state.

During the 1970s, many guerrilla movements emerged in Colombia. One of those groups, the FARC, grew bigger and stronger and eventually became the largest and best organized guerrilla movement in Colombia. The guerrillas eventually became involved in the drug trade, hired as guards for the cartel labs, helping to move drugs for them, or trafficking the drugs themselves.

Jesus Ruiz Henao: "One of my eldest brothers (Francisco) was caught in the middle of the Trujillo Massacre, and he was very badly injured. Francisco had signed up for military service at the age of eighteen before joining a guerrilla group. Luckily, he managed to escape through the mountains and over a river, and after that, he flew to the United Kingdom, where he was granted political asylum. He died of cancer in London in 2017 at age sixty-two."

In the Trujillo Massacre, after being tortured, the hapless victims were dismembered via chainsaws and thrown in the Cauca River, which runs through the town. The killings were carried out by the Cali Cartel and paramilitary groups with the complicity of the local police.

Cocaine and the guerrillas were a part of Jesus' growing up. Cocaine is a powerful drug found in the leaves of the coca shrub, a plant grown primarily in the South American countries of Colombia, Peru, and Bolivia. Cocaine was first extracted from coca leaves in Germany in 1855 by a chemist named Friedriche Gaedecke, who named the ingredient erythroxyline. Four years later, Albert Niemann isolated the compound and renamed it cocaine.

In the 1960s, cocaine was viewed as the "champagne of drugs, meaning it was the choice for the rich and famous." But by the late 1970s, cocaine use, particularly in the US, had skyrocketed.

Ruiz Henao: "My first memory is being seven years old and transporting about five kilos of cocaine every weekend to Trujillo. This, I later discovered, was how my father, along with all the other farmers in the area, paid the guerrillas for protection. The guerrillas had fought the Colombian government for years, but in the 1960s, they were weak. So they were forced to turn to more desperate measures to fight their battles. The guerrillas tried to intimidate my father and the other farmers. They stole what they could and were often violent toward them.

"My father and other farmers felt they had to do something. They were poor and did not have much money. But they did have cocaine. At this point cocaine was not yet in huge demand, but the farmers recognized its value. So the farmers banded together, agreeing that each farmer would produce five kilos of cocaine to help pay for the men and the weapons. They would deliver the goods to the council in the city of Cali, the region's major city. Our council went to the Cali City Council and sold them the cocaine."

Interestingly, this symbiotic relationship between the farmers, Trujillo, and the Cali leaders would eventually give rise to the formation of the Cali Cartel, the drug organization many analysts believe is history's most powerful.

Ruiz Henao: "Each week I would go with our father and two of my brothers, climbing down the hills and across a river to a remote area of the family farm. Looking back now, it is obvious that my father had kept his cocaine production a secret from the rest of the family.

"Hidden among the trees was a freestanding, ramshackle, corrugated-roofed shed. Inside, at the center, was an old oil barrel drum. One of us children would stir the drum's contents. Water was fed down from the river by bamboo shoots. After twenty or so minutes, my father would shout the name of one of us who was not stirring to take over and stir. We children did not know what we were doing until we were much older.

"We did what our father told us because he was a really cruel, strict man, and we feared him. Sometimes, when he got angry, he would use the flat of a machete to spank one of us children when we got out of line. The lives of my brothers and sisters and I were disciplined and hard. We would have to milk the cows and then make the one-and-half-hour journey to school.

"Every Sunday, we traveled by horseback into Trujillo. The round trip would take us about five hours. Once in town, we would tie the horses near the local market, and go and sit near a lady who sold coffee, water, and sweet cakes. A butcher, who never acknowledged me, would remove the package from the horse's saddlebag and replace it with a similar-sized package. At the time, I did not know what the package contained, and I really did not care.

"From a young age, I developed a taste for the finer things in life. I wanted to be on my own. I wanted to make money and buy my own car. One day, I was staring at a large red Toyota pickup when a young girl, not much older than me, who looked like she had money, asked me what I was staring at. I told the girl: 'I'm going to have a car like that someday.' She laughed at me and said: 'You won't ever be able to buy a car like that. You are just a farmer's boy.' Most people would shrink with embarrassment, but I took it as a challenge. 'Watch me,' I told her. I often dreamt about all the things I would buy when I became rich.

"At this point, I did not have any criminal aspirations, even though I did notice that cocaine trafficking was becoming big. I knew people who had made money at it.

"My father died of cancer and my mother could not keep up the farm. Ana Henao, my grandmother, was a rich woman. About 1974, she brought my family from Trujillo to a city called Armenia. The area was controlled by Carlos Lehder, a half German, half Colombian drug trafficker. Later I would learn he was a pioneer in cocaine smuggling to the US."

Born in 1949, Lehder rose from a struggling, small-time pot dealer to become a major godfather in the Medellín Cartel, the crime syndicate largely responsible for initiating the cocaine epidemic plaguing Western society since the late 1970s. One federal US prosecutor, Robert Merkle, said that Lehder "was to cocaine transportation what Henry Ford was to automobiles" because he was the mastermind behind the transportation network that revolutionized the international drug trade.

Before Lehder got involved with drug trafficking in a big way, traffickers smuggled their poison mainly through individual couriers, or so-called mules. Lehder's genius was to devise a sophisticated transportation system that allowed the Medellín Cartel, in the late 1970s and early to mid-1980s, to use Norman's Cay in the Bahamas to transport huge quantities of cocaine from Colombia, the source country, to the US, the world's major illegal drug market.

Lehder commanded a squadron of airplanes that brought in multi-ton loads of cocaine into the US from his base in the Bahamas. By 1987, the DEA and the Colombian government had put Lehder's net wealth at more than three billion dollars. A great admirer of both Nazi icon Adolph Hitler and Marxist Che Guevara, Lehder hated the US and viewed cocaine as a kind of atomic bomb that could destroy Uncle Sam from within. He also aspired to someday become president of Colombia, and he used his illicit fortune to finance his political ambitions.

Lehder retreated to Colombia after a DEA raid on Norman's Cay in 1980. He settled in Armenia and became a local celebrity. He started spreading money around his home turf and around Quindio, the state where Armenia is located. He opened *Posada Alemana*, a huge tourist complex, discotheque, and convention center. Lehder built a statue of John Lennon at the entrance. It had a bullet hole in it.

Ruiz Henao: "I admired Carlos Lehder and the hotel he built, called *Posada Alemana*. I used to visit it many times but did not meet Lehder. I liked his lifestyle and the way he was living. I knew he made his money from cocaine trafficking.

"It was not easy to get into the drug game. Many people wanted to do that. But I had saved money, about three million pesos (about one thousand dollars) and I wanted to break in. I hooked up with a very old man. We had an old car and would go round the jungle and buy three to five kilos of cocaine. We would put the cocaine in the car, drive about five to seven hours, and then go back to the city where we sold it, doubling our profit. I would do this about once a month. It was like having a second job. I could see the drug trade was getting huge, and there was great opportunity in it."

Ruiz Henao's entry into the drug trade was timely. Colombia's role in the international drug trade had shifted from a grower/exporter of marijuana in the early to mid-1970s to a processor/shipper of cocaine in the early 1980s. Ruiz Henao would become one of the estimated six hundred thousand Colombians connected legally or illegally in some way to the cocaine trade, which pumped billions into the Colombian economy.

Fabio Ochoa Sr. had gotten his start in crime by smuggling whiskey and home electronics. In 1978, Pablo Escobar convinced Ochoa to use his well-established and well-connected smuggling routes for the more profitable drug business.

18 April 1981 was a key date in the Medellín Cartel's establishment. Pablo Escobar, Carlos Lehder, and the Ochoa clan met to discuss ways to transport cocaine to the US. By the end of the year, the Medellín Cartel had supervised thirty-eight shipments to the US, containing about nineteen tons of cocaine.

At this time, the Cali Cartel, founded by the brothers Gilberto and Miguel Rodríguez-Orejuela, played a secondary role in the Colombian drug trade. In the mid-1970s, while the more powerful Medellín cartel was establishing a strong base in Miami, the Cali Cartel moved into the New York market. The *Norte del Valle* Cartel, with whom Ruiz Henao would become affiliated, did not exist at this time.

Ruiz Henao: "When I was seventeen, I was sent to live with two aunts in Pereira, a city in west-central Colombia, situated in the western foothills of the Cordillera Central, above the Cauca River Valley. A few months later, I got a job as a postman. I liked it, and I liked being outside among people moving about their daily activity. In the morning, before I delivered the mail, we had to sort it. While I was sorting the mail at the post office, a medium-size envelope dropped to the floor. When I picked it up, I noticed it was partially open and there was a green bill inside. It looked like money, although I didn't really look at it. I put the envelope on the table and carefully took out the bill and put it in my notebook, which I carried with me on postal rounds.

"When I was doing my postal rounds, I took the notebook out and had a good look at the bill. I couldn't believe it. It was a $100 American money bill that somebody had sent through the mail. I had never seen so much money in my life. I said to myself: 'Someday, I will have lots of hundred dollars bills and be rich.'

"Later, I was introduced to a Don Pedro, a very rich man about fifty years old, who lived in Armenia and was connected to the drug business. He needed somebody to drive for him. I got to know Don Pedro well, and he became an important person in my life. One day, I went with him to Cartago in the *Valle del Norte*, about a twenty-minute drive from Pereira to visit one of Don Pedro's friends, a man named Orlando Arcangel Henao, aka *El Mocho* (the Amputee)."

El Mocho would become a top leader of the *Norte del Valle* Cartel. He was arrested on 10 January 2004, in Panama and extradited to New York. Arcangel was the brother of Orlando Henao Montoya, aka *El Hombre del Overol* (the Overalls Man), a former policeman, who became a big man in the drug trade of the *Norte del Valle* Cartel. Henao Montoya surrendered to the Colombian authorities in 1997, but continued to operate from prison, launching attacks against the remnants of the Cali Cartel and associates who were cooperating with the US authorities. In 1998, Montoya was murdered in prison in retaliation for a hit on Cali Cartel chief Helmer Pacho Herrera, supposedly due to concerns that he was cooperating with the DEA.

Ruiz Henao: "In 1980, I met two friends in Pereira, Pedro and Jose, who would become a big influence on my life. We were all ambitious and wanted to make money. We thought drugs would be the way to do it. We went into the jungle around Pereira and found a cocaine wholesale seller who was willing to deal with us youngsters. We bought our first kilo for eight hundred pesos and sold it ourselves. We made nearly fifteen hundred pesos, doubling the amount we paid for it.

"Jose and I came from poor backgrounds, but Pedro was from a rich family. Ironically, Pedro's father became a driving force behind our drug-smuggling venture. He would give Pedro thousands of pesos and told him to go pay the family's bills. Pedro decided he would use his father's money as a 'loan', and with it, he, Jose and I bought larger and larger quantities of cocaine to sell.

"We quickly became Pereira's biggest drug dealers, known for selling a good product at a fair price. Pedro, however, was tardy in paying some of his father's bills. He paid one bill three days late, and his father noticed. Pedro's father questioned him about the late payment. Pedro claimed he forgot. His father beat Pedro, but Pedro took it and did not change his story. His father eventually came around and believed him.

"We dealt drugs for nearly three years and were making good money at it. But being under the thumb of his father, Pedro grew increasingly frustrated. He wanted to be his own man. One day, Pedro told us that we were going to expand our drug-trafficking operation to Italy where his family had contacts in the Sicilian Mafia."

Sicily is an island in the Mediterranean Sea, between North Africa and the Italian mainland. The Mafia, a network of organized crime groups based in Italy and America, evolved over centuries in Sicily. During the early part of the twentieth century, the Sicilian Mafia flourished, expanding its criminal empire and becoming, by the 1970s, a major player in international narcotics trafficking. The Sicilian Mafia dominated the heroin market, but Pedro thought that they might want to get into the emerging cocaine market.

Ruiz Henao: "In September 1982, I agreed to go to Italy and talk with our Sicilian Mafia contact. I was a young lad, about twenty-two years old, but I was not really nervous. I looked at the trip as an adventure. I was getting out of Colombia and going to experience something new. I liked that.

"I took a flight to Rome, Italy. When I met with the Mafia contact, he was surprised to meet such a young gangster. I was a little nervous. I was just a country boy without much life experience. Besides, I did not understand Italian. But Spanish is a Romance language like Italian, so I was able to make out okay.

"The Mafia man liked what I told him, and saw perhaps a European connection for our proposal. I could tell why the Sicilian Mafia was the world's most powerful criminal organization. Pedro's contact had vision. He could see the future. He wanted to know if I could go to the United Kingdom and meet with one of his representatives. I agreed to go.

"At that time, getting into the United Kingdom was easy. Upon arriving, they asked you how long you wanted to stay and stamped your visa into your passport. There was really no worry about drug trafficking in the United Kingdom in 1985.

"I flew from Rome and arrived at London's Heathrow airport. I picked up a taxi that took me to the Russell Square area of Central London. I walked to an Italian restaurant that was just around the corner and asked for Bruno, the man I was supposed to see. After introductions, Bruno took me to the back of the restaurant and his office and offered me a drink.

"Bruno and a friend, who was there with him, were very sociable and a lot talking went on. They discussed opening up the United Kingdom for cocaine."

In the early 1980s, the UK market for cocaine was small, reveals Pete Walsh, an expert on the British drug trade and War on Drugs and the author of *Drug War: The Secret History*.

Pete Walsh: "Cocaine had not really taken off (in the UK) up to that point because it was expensive and difficult to acquire. The cheaper stimulant, amphetamine, or 'speed,' was much more popular, particularly among working-class or blue-collar users. Cultural markers can be important in promoting drug use and speed was associated with punk rock music, as well as a cult, all-night dance scene in parts of the UK known as Northern soul.

"Speed had the advantage that it could be manufactured domestically from chemicals, and so did not involve complex, costly, and risky importations from far away. Still, cocaine was obtainable, particularly among the wealthier young and among denizens of the pop and rock world – musicians, roadies, venue owners, promoters, hangers-on – some of whom had contacts in the United States, where the market was much more mature.

"By the mid-1970s, the American star Randy Newman complained that usage of 'nose candy' was even heavier in London than in Los Angeles. This was certainly an exaggeration, but it makes the point that coke was available among a well-connected subset of society. But it had not yet taken off as a mass-market product because of price, scarcity and the fact that there were no established distribution channels for it: if you managed to smuggle a couple of kilos of coke into the United Kingdom, who would you sell it to?"

Ruiz Henao: "Bruno and his associate took me to a pub for a beer, and later we went to a hotel, where I checked in. The next day at about 10 a.m., they came to my hotel room and handed me a small suitcase. I was told at the bottom of the suitcase, between the suitcase walls, was money: seventy thousand pounds. Later, we went to a coffee shop, and they explained to me how to start sending small amounts of cocaine through the post. Bruno's friend gave me a list of seven different places to where we would be sending the dope. I stayed in the United Kingdom for about a week. Then they put me in a black cab to Heathrow, and I flew back to Colombia.

"But before I left, I went to certain areas of the city at night time and hung around the nightclubs, staying up to three in the morning. I saw drugs being consumed. I observed how they sold the drugs and who would buy them. I could tell there would be a market for cocaine. I left England very excited.

"I didn't tell anybody in my family about my drug trafficking plans. I kept it a secret. My family was very conservative and religious, devoutly Catholic, and went to church every Sunday. They would not have approved. I prayed every single night and tried to be a good Catholic, but I wanted to live a nice lifestyle, and I knew I could get it through the drug trade."

Interestingly, Ruiz Henao dealt with Italian drug traffickers, at least during the initial period of his involvement with the British drug trade. Pete Walsh explains that the Sicilian Mafia and its US cousin La Cosa Nostra have never been much of a phenomenon in the United Kingdom: their power has always been focused on Italy and North America. However, in this key period, they were, for a short time, an important presence in England.

Walsh: "One group of Italians, based in West London and with links to the Sicilian Mafia town of Acireale, imported large amounts of cannabis and were also known to distribute cocaine. They were identified and targeted in a HM Customs and Excise (HMCE) investigation called Operation Conquest in 1982. Scotland Yard's Murder Squad also became involved when one of their associates, Sergio Vaccari, was stabbed to death at his flat in London in September 1982. In the end, the gang's leader was jailed for eight years.

"The actual overlords of the Mafia in the United Kingdom were two other men: Alfonso Caruana and his ally, Francesco Di Carlo. The Caruana brothers were major Sicilian drug traffickers who were well established in Canada, Venezuela, and elsewhere. Alfonso moved to an affluent area of Surrey, a county just outside London. There, he ran his criminal operation. Among other investments, his group soon acquired a hotel, a travel agency, a *bureau de change,* and a wine bar in London.

"Caruana and Di Carlo undoubtedly had strong connections in cocaine source countries, but whether that included Colombians at this time – as opposed to, say, Peruvians or Bolivians – I do not know. They were targeted in another HM Customs drug probe, Operation Devotion, in

1985. This was mainly concerned with cannabis and heroin, but also encompassed a startling seizure of forty-seven kilos of cocaine (a huge amount for Europe at the time) in Hamburg Harbor, Germany, in May 1984. This was believed to be bound for the United Kingdom.

"Di Carlo was eventually arrested and jailed for twenty-five years in London, but Caruana escaped and went on to become a hugely influential international trafficker."

Ruiz Henao had worked out a deal in the United Kingdom.

Ruiz Henao: "I came back to Colombia to tell my partners the good news. We would deliver the cocaine to England, a real open market where we believed law enforcement was lax. We were going to start out with just a five-kilo delivery, but we realized that we had no contacts in the United Kingdom. We had no way of getting the cocaine there.

"We negotiated with the Sicilian Mafia for a couple of weeks. Finally, they agreed that they would deliver the product to one of their contacts in Barcelona, Spain, and then move it to the United Kingdom. We found a cruise liner that made regular trips to Barcelona. We would use that method as our means of delivery. We were nervous, but we knew to get ahead in life we had to take chances.

"Jose and I took with us five kilos of cocaine, a five day supply of food, and enough water, got into a small boat, and made our way to the cruise liner. We snuck aboard and stowed away on the ship. When we reached Spain, we jumped the ship and swam to shore. We made it with no problem.

"The Sicilian Mafia was really impressed with us. We worked out a deal where we would smuggle five kilos of cocaine once a month. We bought the cocaine at a thousand dollars per kilo and sold it to the Mafia for twenty thousand a kilo. We were in business but just getting started.

"It was a lot of work, though, and somebody might ask why we did not tap the US market instead? After all, the Medellín and Cali Cartels were focusing their drug smuggling efforts on the US market and were smuggling cocaine by the ton. The truth is I was afraid of America and its power. I realized at a young age that I would never do business there. I could see how the US was clamping down on the drug trade."

The Reagan administration (1980-1989) pushed ahead, in the early 1980s, with a hardline agenda for its War on Drugs which emphasized tough military action. In launching its War on Drugs in 1982, President Regan reorganized the chain of command and sent an impressive array of military hardware, intelligence, and other resources to South Florida and the front line in the drug battle. Congress strongly supported the Reagan administration and calls for a tougher stance on the War on Drugs came from a variety of legislative sources, including the powerful House Foreign Affairs Committee and the House Select Committee on Narcotics Control. Latin America became the focus of Uncle Sam's anti-drug efforts, and the War on Drugs shifted from heroin to marijuana and cocaine.

Ruiz Henao: "I have never gone to America, not even for a short time. After my trip to Italy, I looked toward the United Kingdom and Europe because it was an untapped market. The anti-drug controls the British had in place were weak. Colombians were starting to go to the United Kingdom. It was easy to get in. If you got caught, the prison sentences were not as tough as the ones they had in the US. So we had ample manpower from whom to draw. I was ready to go."

In the United Kingdom, drug use and abuse was rising by the early 1980s. Heroin was the predominant drug of choice. In the 1960s, seizures of illicitly imported heroin were insignificant. The first major seizure of smuggled heroin came in 1971 when 1.14 kilograms were seized. In

1984, Customs seized 312 kilograms and the police seized a further 49 kilograms.

Cocaine was first made illegal by the Dangerous Drug Act of 1920 in the United Kingdom. It is now classed as a Class A drug controlled by the Misuse of Drugs Act of 1971. Possession carries punishment of up to seven years in prison, an unlimited fine, or both. Cocaine is legal for medical use as a local anesthetic.

At Christmas time in 1979, drug lord Pablo Escobar visited Pereira. Escobar had rapidly become the world's most notorious gangster. Born on 1 December 1949, in the Colombian city of Rionegro, Antioquia, Escobar came from a modest background. His father worked as a peasant farmer while his mother was a school teacher. Escobar, from an early age, had the ambition to raise himself up from his humble beginnings. He reportedly began his life of crime early, starting by stealing tombstones and cars, and then moving into the cigarette smuggling business.

In the mid-1970s, Escobar helped found the crime organization that later became known as the Medellín Cartel.

Ruiz Henao: "At first, I thought Escobar was legitimate. He was giving houses and other things to the people. His reputation was impeccable. He was like an idol. Gradually it came out that he a big-time drug dealer."

The Medellín Cartel focused largely on the production, transport, and sale of cocaine. By the late 1970s, Escobar was portraying himself as a kind of Robin Hood who helped the poor.

"I heard Pablo was in town, so I went to see him. There was a big crowd around him. People were excited. I managed to muscle my way to the front of the line. He was known to give gifts to the people. He handed me a bicycle and shook my hand. I couldn't believe it. A bicycle from Pablo Escobar!

"I know the British press later called me the 'Pablo Escobar of the United Kingdom drug trade,' but I was nothing like him. Pablo started off as a good man, but I think the power and money he accumulated turned him into a bad man. He became violent and almost destroyed Colombia. I never wanted to harm people. They say I killed people with my drug trafficking business. I never forced anybody to take drugs. They came to me, and I sold them drugs. I never made them do anything against their will. It was their choice."

TWO

GETTING ESTABLISHED

Jesus Ruiz Henao arrived back in Colombia at the end of 1982. It had been an amazing and productive trip.

Ruiz Henao: "I gave Pedro the suitcase with the money, which he passed on to one of his workers. He gave me five thousand pounds for taking the trip. It's hard to change the pounds into Colombian money, mainly because not many institutions or people in Colombia wanted pounds. In the end, I managed to change the money at a Republic Bank.

"Pedro, Jose, and I all agreed we would begin to send cocaine to the United Kingdom. We started with small amounts of three hundred to four hundred grams, although at one time we did send eight hundred grams. We created a company address and started to send envelopes overseas. To not attract attention, we did not include cocaine in every mailing. We sent the dope in parcels about once every month. We did this for a couple of years and were successful.

"The amount of money we made was small compared to what we would make later. When we started to get going, we were making about ten thousand pounds a month. There were expenses, of course, particularly bribes. We also had to pay off the people at the post office."

The United Kingdom authorities were aware that Colombia had become a major processing and distribution center for cocaine. Using x-ray equipment, the UK authorities started to monitor letter and parcels sent from Colombia. Interestingly, much of the mail sent from Colombia was contaminated with cocaine residue.

Ruiz Henao: "We were cautious and not greedy, so it was very difficult to trace the shipments back to us. I can recall maybe two or three times when a shipment did not go through."

In late 1983, Bruno, Ruiz Henao's United Kingdom contact, came to Colombia with a large sum of money to pay for a drug shipment. They were to be met by the Colombians to whom they owed the money, but the Colombians never showed up. Bruno and his associates got tired of waiting and decided to head back to the United Kingdom. But they were intercepted by police, who arrested them and seized the money.

The Colombians who were owed the money needed an explanation. They felt Ruiz Henao was responsible for the lost money since he had recommended Bruno and his associates. It was a very dangerous time for Ruiz Henao, especially when *El Mono Flechas*, a well-known contract killer, contacted him and told him they needed to arrange a meeting. Flechas was working for a man named Cebas, to whom the British owed the money.

Ruiz Henao: "I was wondering what to do when one day I looked out the second-floor window and saw three men standing outside and looking toward my window. I realized they were *sicarios*, that is, contract killers. I was being watched. I decided that I had to confront the situation before it became worse.

"I agreed to meet with Cebas. I traveled by bus to Calarcá, a small town close to Armenia, to explain to him what had happened. I was very nervous. You could not mess with these killers. They were really dangerous. I had no choice. If I didn't meet, I would have been hunted down and killed. The British had told their Colombian sellers that they would not pay them again.

"The following day, I wrote details about myself on a piece of paper—who I was, whom to contact if someone found the note—and stuffed the paper under my testicles. In case I was murdered, I could be identified. The cartels had murdered many hundreds of Colombians and dumped their bodies in rivers. No one knew who they were. I did not want that to happen to me.

"When I reached the town, I went to a public phone and called the man who had contacted me. I was told to stay put and somebody would come for me. Some men in a Mitsubishi came and picked me up. We drove to a warehouse on the outskirts of town, where another two men jumped into the car. We drove close to a river where we stopped, and I was told to get out of the car. I was shaking and thinking of my loved ones. But I got strong and kept my head. I was on my own. I was the only person who could save me. I decided to be aggressive. I told them I did nothing wrong and demanded: 'Why are you doing this?' No one answered me.

"Then a car arrived. I was put in the car and taken to see Cebas, who was waiting for me in a villa nearby. Cebas ran a big cocaine trafficking organization in Spain and Holland. He was murdered in Armenia in 2000, ironically, by a contract killer. I stood in front of Cebas, trying to control myself as he glared at me. He was a stone-cold killer, and I had to be careful how I talked to him.

"I tried to explain what had happened, but he didn't give me a chance. He told me he was sick and tired of hearing excuses from me and wanted his money. He would not kill me if I made restitution to him. I assured him that I would pay him. Cebas left the meeting. He sent his people to my home with me. I had to hand over my car and the deed to my home. It really set me back financially. It took a little time, about three years, but I did pay off the debt. I was very lucky. I could have been another victim of Colombia's drug war.

"The debt drained me. I had to nearly start all over again. I went to see a drug dealer in Pereira, who I knew was making a drug shipment to Europe in about two months. I persuaded him to include a small drug load from me as part of the shipment. I managed to scrape the money together to pay for the shipment. A gangster named Lubin heard about my transaction. He had not been allowed in the deal and was pissed. He thought I was deliberately cutting him out. He started spreading stories about me—how I was a liar, penniless, and couldn't be trusted. He raised such a fuss that I heard the man with whom I had arranged the drug shipment was having second thoughts about taking my shipment.

"I was furious. I got a gun and went looking for Lubin. I found him at a boutique shop. I yelled at him. 'Hey, man, what the hell are you trying to do to me? I know you got a gun. I got a gun here.' Then I rolled up my shirt and showed him the gun on my waistband. I continued: 'I know you have killed many, but come outside and let's settle this.'

"Those in the shop either ran outside or got down on the floor. Lubin started to walk toward me. I was nervous. I started to reach for my gun. Then he said: 'No one is going to be happy if I kill you here. Let's do it another day.' Lubin left. Nothing ever happened, and I was able to get back into the drug business."

Rubiela, Jesus's older sister, introduced Jesus to a man named Hugo. Hugo was articulate and knowledgeable about the drug business.

"Hugo knew how to transport large quantities of cocaine from Colombia to Europe. Hugo told me about how he had helped arrange a two-million-dollar deal. I was very impressed and decided to work with him. We arranged for a cocaine shipment to Europe. Initially, it looked like everything had gone to plan. Hugo told me that the shipment had arrived in the United Kingdom with no problem.

"About a week later, however, Hugo came to me and said the shipment had been seized by the police. I didn't believe Hugo and suspected something was wrong. I began to make inquiries to all my connections in Europe. It took a few weeks, but we discovered the truth. Hugo had never sent the shipment. Hugo had used the drugs to pay off a large debt he owed to a powerful drug trafficking organization in Medellin.

"I personally went looking for Hugo. I left a lot of messages for him, including a couple with his sister. One night in a car port, someone started shooting at me as I returned to my car. I was shot in the stomach, but I still managed to get to a house, where I was kindly let in. The shooters ran away. To avoid any police inquiries, I went to a private doctor to have the wound treated. The doctor said I was lucky to be alive. It was obvious to me that Hugo had hired *sicarios* to kill me. I knew it was only a matter of time before he would try again. I had to find Hugo before he found me.

"The man, who ran the lab that produced the stolen drugs and to whom I had to pay for the missing drugs, offered me the services of his own *sicarios* to sort out the situation so that he could be paid. A little while later, three trucks filled with well-armed *sicarios* went to Medellín to find Hugo. They had an informant who told them that Hugo was now under the protection of a very powerful government official. If they were to find and kill Hugo, there would be all-out war. The *sicarios* were out of their element in Medellín and at a huge disadvantage. Reluctantly, they returned to Pereira.

"The problem with Hugo did not go away. He continued to be protected, and I continued to be out of the money he owed me. I decided that it would be wise to let things calm down. But the producer of the cocaine began to pressure me for his money. I knew I had to pay. I was responsible for the loss. So I sold some of my property to pay the debt.

"On the sixth of December 1985, I got married to a woman named Maria Isabel Londoño. Maria was a neighbor, and we had dated for over five years. It was time to get married. Maria is an incredible woman, very loyal and happy. She is always positive. I never saw her in a bad mood, even when I was busted. We traveled to Bogotá and then to Madrid, where we spent a few days before moving to Paris, France. We rented an apartment in central Paris and lived there for a couple of months. It was really peaceful.

"In mid-1986, we decided to move to the United Kingdom. My sister had been living in the Camden Town area of London for some years. The area was popular with Colombians."

Colombians were a part of the political refugees who, in the 1960s and 1970s, started arriving in the UK. And with the Colombians came cocaine.

Walsh: "It seems to have first become apparent to British law enforcement in late 1973 that cocaine use was increasing and that Colombia had emerged as a processing and distribution center (it wasn't yet important as a coca-growing region). That year and into 1974, the DEA reportedly arrested fifteen people said to be trafficking to London, Miami, and Montreal. Various people involved in smuggling to London were identified as a result of this DEA investigation, and a British Customs analyst concluded: 'It is clear from the reports we have received that there was a highly organized traffic in cocaine from Bogotá with international connections.'

"To halt this traffic, HMCE conducted a secret exercise at London's Heathrow Airport in September and October of 1974, focusing on passengers flying to or from the South American cities of Bogotá, La Paz, Lima, and Santiago. Surprisingly, they found nothing, and closed the operation down.

"But then, over the following two months, three seizures of unusually high purity cocaine were made at the airport in false-bottomed suitcases, including a new record of four kilos. Each one originated in Colombia. One of them was carried by an Englishwoman who had flown from Bogotá via Zurich. 'Within three weeks, we had two very similar seizures and you start to realize that you have been missing it,' a former Customs officer told me. 'The cartels are clever people. They won't send couriers direct from Colombia. They sent that particular one through Switzerland and to a mature English woman. That opened my eyes.' Inquiries led to the identification of two Colombians living in London who had recruited the woman. Both men were believed to be active traffickers with contacts in Paris, Madrid, and Zurich.

"The UK at this stage seems to have been supplied mainly by three types of cocaine smuggler: (I) British-born freelancers, who bought the drug for themselves or pooled resources with a handful of other dealers and were prepared to fly to source countries or pay couriers to do so; (II) South American nationals living in the United Kingdom, including students; and (III) South Americans, US citizens, and Canadians who transited in the UK from South America, bound for the USA.

"The main impetus was coming from the Colombians, who were pushing their product and acting as market-makers. They also used the letter post, mailing small but regular amounts of powder to recipients among the Colombian community of West London, many of whom lived in cramped serviced apartments and worked in the hotel trade. HM Customs monitored letters and parcels to these apartments and used a small x-ray cabinet to see inside them. They found that much of the mail from South America was contaminated. 'It was only grams but we got a huge amount of intelligence because there were letters with this stuff, so we began to understand what was happening in the cocaine market,' one of the officers involved told me.

"One young Colombian, Julio Barrera, favored the posting of hollowed-out books with coke hidden inside. He also called on the services of a roving gang of pickpockets from his native country, which was known to swarm through airport security gates carrying contraband; their activities came to an abrupt end when they were arrested for burgling hotel rooms in London. Barrera was responsible for the biggest seizure of 1975, of 2.45 kilos, using a female British courier, who flew to Paris to collect flake from a Colombian accomplice, then returned with it hidden in a suitcase. She was already under observation, leading to Barrera's arrest.

"But Customs was still finding only small quantities of narcotics. Partly this was because powder was much easier to conceal than cannabis, and partly because no one was yet bringing in bulk shipments; certainly nothing like the amounts that would prevail in just a few years' time.

"The smugglers were also hard to spot: they usually dressed smartly, spoke well, and had legitimate-sounding reasons for travelling abroad. They also constantly adapted their methods. The government claimed that the United Kingdom had 'a relatively stable situation as far as narcotic drug dependence is concerned.' Its principal concern remained not cocaine or heroin, but cannabis, which was routinely arriving in bulk."

Following the early arrivals, more Colombians began arriving in search of employment or to escape the political situation in their country. Most Colombians in the UK settled in or around London, where they are generally dispersed. However, a small concentration resided in the boroughs of Lambeth, Islington, Southwark, and Camden. Many Colombians came to work in the UK on visas, mainly in the domestic services and catering industries. Historically, the UK has, in fact, proven the most popular European destination for Colombian migrants despite the lack of historical links evident with Spain.

Ruiz Henao: "We initially got a one-month visa, but then we applied for and got a one-year visa. I bought my first property in the United Kingdom on Arlington Road.

Colombia had become a basket case with the drug violence, so I thought it unwise to drug deal."

The violence in Colombia was indeed epidemic. During the Colombian drug trade's formative period, the Cali and Medellín Cartels operated in their home country with virtual impunity. However, by the mid-1980s, the United States government was pressuring Colombia to abandon its laissez-faire policy. President Reagan had declared the War on Drugs in 1982, and the US shifted the focus of its interdiction efforts from heroin in Asia to cocaine in Latin America. Uncle Sam recognized Colombia as the hub of the region's drug trade.

Two years later, Rodrigo Lara Bonilla, Colombia's justice minister, reopened the case involving Pablo Escobar's arrest in 1976 on drug possession charges. Escobar was, at the time, serving as an alternate delegate to the Colombia Congress, but he had higher political aspirations. When the 1976 case was reopened, Don Pablo, as many now respectfully called the drug baron, suddenly found himself in the harsh and uncomfortable glare of public scrutiny.

Stripped away was the image of Don Pablo, leading citizen. Exposed was the reality: Pablo Escobar, drug lord. Escobar sued Lara Bonilla for libel, sniffing, "I'm a victim of a persecution campaign," but eventually dropped out of public life, humiliated and fixated on revenge. Lara Bonilla received death threats, but ignored them. He was determined to investigate Escobar and go after the country's mafia. In 1984, he authorized the spectacular raid on *Tranquilandia*, the major cocaine processing plant in the Amazon region. He paid for it with his life, for a few months later, *sicarios* machine-gunned him to death on a residential street in Bogotá.

The justice minister's murder compelled President Belisario Betancur to declare a "war without quarter" against all drug traffickers, and the Medellín Cartel godfathers did a disappearing act from public life. The Cali godfathers didn't approve of Lara Bonilla's assassination, but they were forced to go underground as well. That's when Gilberto Rodríguez-Orejuela and his friend Jorge Ochoa left for Spain, and Santacruz traveled to Mexico and sent some of his lieutenants to the United States to investigate possible locations for new cocaine processing labs.

At 11:40 a.m. on 6 November 1985, approximately thirty-five M-19 guerrillas stormed the Colombian Palace of Justice, located on Bogotá's central Plaza de Bolivar. Within minutes, the guerrillas had two hundred and fifty hostages, including Alfonso Reyes Echandia, the chief justice of Colombia's Supreme Court, and many of the twenty-four Supreme Court justices. For the next twenty-four hours, thousands of soldiers and police tried to retake the building, but the heavily-armed and well-entrenched guerrillas fought them off. When the government finally prevailed, twenty-five hostages lay dead, including Chief Justice Reyes, and apparently all the guerrillas.

It is widely believed the Medellín Cartel paid the guerrillas to take the Palace and burn the extradition case files in the court archives, which contained incriminating evidence against them. The justices, many of who favored upholding the extradition treaty with the United States, were scheduled to vote on the issue in the near future. The shocking attack on the heart of the Colombian legal system set the tenor for the rest of the decade.

Escobar and his allies elevated their terror campaign to another level, murdering leading presidential candidate Luis Carlos Galan, despite his sixteen bodyguards. Many Colombians believed the charismatic Galan would win the 1990 election and continue Barco's tough policy toward drug trafficking. Galan's death was a turning point. Using his powers under the state of siege, Colombian President Virgilio Barco reinstated the US/Colombia extradition treaty, which the Colombian courts had suspended, and launched an all-out war against the Medellín Cartel. Between mid-

August and mid-December 1989, the government arrested 497 people, seized $250 million in drugs and property, and extradited nine suspects to the US. Escobar struck back during the same period, killing 187 officials and civilians, carrying out 205 bombings, and causing $501 million in damage.

And the terror continued.

Ruiz Henao: "The violence of the Colombian drug trade was incredible. If I had stayed in Colombia, I would be dead. The violence is something that stays with you every single day. You wake up and say to yourself: 'If I get up today, am I going to get caught or I'm going to get a bullet?' It would be one or the other. Most of the people I knew thirty to forty years ago are dead or in prison in Colombia or the United States.

"When you enter the drug trade, you think you need to use force or violence to survive. I told my boys that they could use violence to protect our interests. I did not want to go to prison. I thought it would be better if I died. But surprisingly, I did not have to use violence. I never killed anybody and never told anybody to kill someone. I had temptation, of course, but I never followed through. I believe it's a sin to go against God's law and to do something against somebody's will.

"In Colombia, you carried a gun. You had to if you were a drug dealer. But that was not the case in the United Kingdom, where the gun laws are very strict. It is nearly impossible to carry a gun, although I must admit I did carry one.

"I only had to pull my gun out once. I was driving a car in Colombia and had a girl beside me. We stopped at a traffic light. In the rearview mirror, I saw the man in the car behind me, with a gun, get out of his car and walk towards my car. When he came up to me, I opened the door, jumped out, and pointed my gun at him, I said: 'Come on, you want to do it.' He put the gun away, went back to his car, and drove off."

By 1990, more than two hundred court officials and at least forty Colombian judges had been murdered. Colombian President Virgilio Barco, who took office in 1986, implemented the Colombia–United States extradition treaty. The Medellín Cartel responded by launching a ruthless terrorist campaign against the state.

Calling themselves "the Extraditables," the cartel vowed "better a grave in Colombia than a jail in the United States" and began to target prominent supporters of extradition, as well as get-tough-on-drugs officials.

Ruiz Henao: "I had had enough with the violence. So in mid-1986, I emigrated to the United Kingdom. At the time, it was very easy to stay in the UK. Now, after my case, they changed the rules, making it tougher. The newspapers said I came in 1990, but I was well established in England before then. You really can't believe everything you read in the media. I believe about sixty percent of it is true and forty percent is rubbish."

Pete Walsh says the British drug scene at that time was entering what he would call its second phase.

Walsh: "Its first phase was the novelty period of the mid-sixties to the mid-seventies, when drugs for most people were a new experience. It was a time of social and political transformation, and saw the emergence of the counter culture. Young people were willing to experiment with new ideas and new sensations.

"A lot of the smuggling and dealing was haphazard, even friendly. Adventurous travellers would bring a few pounds of pot back from Morocco or Afghanistan and sell it or hand it out to friends, often for no profit. Eventually some of the 'hippie' smugglers realized that demand was not going away, and started to ship in bigger amounts, often by yachts or small boats from Morocco and Lebanon. The trade became much more commercial and lucrative. But the demand remained mainly for cannabis; hard drugs such as heroin and cocaine were niche products and unlikely to be found in any quantity in most town or cities.

"By the second phase, however, this burgeoning cannabis market was attracting more serious business-minded individuals. Some of them, though by no means all, were violent criminals; many others were just smart, greedy entrepreneurs with an appetite for risk. They took over the trade, made new connections with a wide variety of foreign suppliers, corrupted port workers, police officers, and other officials, and pioneered new methods of importation. It was also the start of the rise of hard drugs: heroin at first, which took off in the cities of Liverpool and Glasgow, both hard hit by rising unemployment, and later, cocaine."

Ruiz Henao: "I had an assortment of jobs. I worked in an Italian coffee shop in the Liverpool Street area, which sold sandwiches. I cleaned offices for Office Care from 1987 to 1991. I worked for British Telecom. My wife attended English language school. We settled in a quiet lifestyle. It was a happy life. I really liked British culture, the people, and the lifestyle. I was fascinated by everything British. We didn't have a lot of money but life was good.

"In December 1988, my daughter was born. It was amazing experience. I can say it was the best day of my life. It was the same thing when my son was born later in 1999. I was excited about having a boy. I now had a boy and girl. It was incredible.

"Gradually, my English improved. I met a lot of people and made several friends. I stayed in contact with Pedro and Jose, my friends in Colombia, and kept abreast of developments in the country. I could not do any work in the drug trade mainly because of the heat on me from Hugo and the people who were protecting him.

"I saved the money I made. I wanted to buy my own flat in London. I stayed small in my drug dealing for a couple of years. I was making two to five thousand pounds a month, small compared what I would make later.

"I went to look up my friend Bruno. The United Kingdom had never proved anything against him about his trip to Colombia, and he made it back to the UK. I found out that Bruno was in ill health and had gone back to Italy.

"I became good friends with an Englishman named Rob. He invited me to his home, where I met his wife and family. We talked about drug trafficking. I told him what I had done. He said he had some good contacts who would be interested in buying cocaine, and he would introduce them to me.

"I was around drugs, but I never got the temptation to use drugs. My parents had educated me about the dangers of illegal drugs. They told us not to touch drugs. So I was wary about using them. None of my ten brothers and sisters touched cocaine, marijuana, or heroin growing up, even though we had lived with coca and marijuana plants around us.

"As for heroin, that is real bad stuff. It can really destroy people. Don't get me wrong. Cocaine can do the same thing, but heroin is much more dangerous. I did some marijuana from Africa, two or three times, in small quantities. It is very difficult to make money smuggling marijuana. It is bulky and the volume is very hard to deal with. Besides, I think smuggling marijuana increases your chances of something going wrong, of getting caught. I once had a chance to bring two or three tons of marijuana into the United Kingdom, but I said no. It would have been a real headache handling it. I know the press reported that the police said marijuana was part of my business, but those reports were wrong.

"As for the other drugs, I know what meth is, but I didn't touch it either. I don't like crack. It is a killer. There is a big difference between cocaine and crack. I know people bought cocaine from us to make crack. It made me sad because they didn't know what they were doing.

"I never touched cocaine until I was forty-two years old and at a party in Brazil. I was on a yacht, partying, and there were lines of cocaine on a table. I tried some for the first time."

One day, Jesus decided he would start selling cocaine again.

"I had been itching to get back into the trade. First, I would do my homework. I began to study the British market for cocaine."

In the mid-1980s, cocaine was not new to the UK. Cocaine, in fact, was a well-established drug among users and one that was favored by the middle class. Ruiz Henao says most of his users were middle-class, respectable citizens, craving for a snort.

"For several months after work, I would do what I did on my first trip to the United Kingdom. I would go to certain areas of the city at night and observe the cocaine being consumed, especially around the night clubs. I would stay until three or four in the morning and watch how they sold the cocaine. They would buy an ounce of cocaine and went back into the nightclub. I decided that cocaine would be very easy to sell. I was convinced more than ever that there was a great opportunity to establish a United Kingdom drug distribution network from Colombia.

"In my research, I quickly discovered how utterly reliant the authorities where on technology. In their investigations, they relied heavily on the use of listening and telecommunication devices. I realized that to be successful in the British drug trade, all I had to do was stay away from technology and from informers. I would communicate the old-fashioned way through human contact and only deal with individuals I fully trusted. I worked directly with people who sold drugs for me. No phones or direct contact with anybody who was selling drugs for me.

"The cops didn't know about me because I didn't use technology to do business. I would use people. I would contact directly with anybody who was selling drugs for me. I kept a very low profile. I didn't go around flashing money.

I enjoyed my vacations in Brazil and Spain, and I spent a lot of money there. But I wouldn't do it in the UK.

"I had two or three good customers. My first cocaine deal was by post. It was so easy to sell it… about five grams of cocaine. I would spend ten British pounds, or about thirty thousand Colombian pesos, to buy the cocaine.

"I treated my drug dealing like a business. As is the case for any good business, you need to find the right people. When I was in Colombia, I was put in situations where my associates were talking about killing somebody. I had to stand up and say: 'That is not me.' The *sicarios* did not like it. Committing killings was a way they made money. It was for that reason that I was in danger in Colombia, and I had to leave or I would be dead. I didn't need to go around killing people. I believed in being smart and clever. I turned down business with people, hundreds of them. They wanted to get into the British drug market, and I was Mr. Big, the person to deal with. But I thought they were too violent. Killing was their first option in doing business. I felt you didn't need to kill people to be successful in the drug trade.

"In keeping with my business philosophy, the people I recruited not only had to be good workers, they had to be trustworthy. I needed to build trust. At the beginning, when I dealt with somebody, I would give him a kilo and say I needed my money for the deal in an hour. Then I would give him five kilos. I would say I need the money today. Then I gave him fifty kilos, and he said he would give me half the money now and the other half when he sold it. I agreed. Then he takes two hundred kilos, and I told him to pay when he was ready. I knew I could trust him. Someone not familiar with the drug dealing thinks the drug trade is cut throat. It's not really. It's built on trust.

"To show you how it works: once, I was told I needed a big van. I went to Liverpool Street in London and to the basement of a bank. The elevator came. It opened and it was full of money from the bank. I filled up my van with over fourteen million pounds. I drove the money to one of my safe houses.

"The people I was dealing with had very high contacts at the bank. I didn't know anything. I just took the money, counted it, and laundered it myself. Selling cocaine is no problem. It's what you can do with money that's the challenge.

"I tried to be honest with my people, and I expected them to be honest with me. I believe that if you try to do anything shifty or underhanded, that bad energy will affect the business. I think that is good business sense and can be applied to any business, legal or illegal. Don't let any dark energy come into your business because things will surely go wrong."

When Ruiz Henao came to the United Kingdom, he lived in a flat. The woman downstairs in the building was a single mother with four children.

By 1993, Ruiz Henao was really focused on his drug business.

Ruiz Henao: "Cocaine use was growing in the UK, and I knew I could make a fortune if I used my head. It looked like things were cooling down in Colombia. So at the end of 1993, I moved my family back to Colombia. I wanted to upgrade my knowledge of the cocaine business and to make the contacts I needed for my growing organization. It was time to move cocaine in serious quantities and to make serious money.

"But just before that providence, I got unbelievably lucky. In 1993, I won the British spot the ball competition, a traditional newspaper promotion. It involves a player having to guess the position of a ball, which has been removed from a photograph of a ball sport, especially association football. I received a £102,000 in prize money. The competition was really popular back then. This is the money the British authorities claimed I used to create my cocaine empire, but it had nothing to do with my drug business."

THREE

THE *SICARIOS*

Around the time of Ruiz Henao's return to Colombia, the country's long-term battle with Pablo Escobar, the so-called world's greatest outlaw, was coming to a head. For nearly a decade, Escobar had launched a narco terrorist campaign that had brought Colombia to its knees. Then Escobar brokered a favorable deal to surrender in 1991 that allowed him to build a prison to his specifications.

Cynical Colombians scoffed and dubbed the prison holding Escobar *La Catedral* (the Cathedral). Escobar's new home stood high on a hill, part of a ten-acre spread that included a soccer field, a gymnasium, a recreational center, a discotheque, a bar, and a sweeping view of the Medellín Valley below. Escobar, in fact, had supervised the prison's construction.

His thousand-square-foot "cell" was bigger than the warden's accommodations, and had a king-size bed and a private bath with Jacuzzi, as well as fine furnishings handpicked by the prisoner.

For company, Escobar had six of his top lieutenants, including his brother Roberto.

The police were not allowed inside the prison, but the press reported comings and goings from the Cathedral at all hours of the day and night. It soon became evident that

Escobar was still running his empire from within the prison walls yet the government did nothing.

When the Colombian authorities attempted to move him to another prison, Escobar escaped and went on the run. On 30 January 1993, a bomb exploded in downtown Bogotá, killing twenty people. The country's public enemy number one had sent a message to the nation.

Then came a shock. The following day, two bombs—one containing an estimated one hundred kilos of dynamite and the other containing eighty kilos—exploded in Medellín in front of apartment buildings where Escobar's wife, two children, his sister, and his mother-in-law were staying. Meanwhile, five men showed up at the weekend country retreat of Escobar's mother, located about forty-five miles from Medellin, ordered the lone caretaker out and blew up the place.

In a communiqué released to the press on 2 February, a new group calling itself *Los Pepes* (Persecuted by Pablo Escobar) claimed responsibility for the attacks. The communiqué declared that *Los Pepes* were working toward "the total elimination of Pablo Escobar, his followers, and his assets to give him a taste of his medicine, which he unfairly dishes out to so many."

Escobar struck back. Mid-morning on 15 February, two powerful bombs exploded five minutes and twelve blocks apart in downtown Bogotá, killing four people and injuring more than a hundred others. The gang war continued tit for tat. Escobar sought to turn himself into the government after his escape under new terms, but no agreement was finalized

The writing, though, was on the wall for Escobar. Colombia's nightmare ended on 2 December 1993, when the alliance of the Colombian National Police, US law enforcement, and *Los Pepes* achieved their objective of poisoning the sea around the big fish. When all the escapes and violence had ended, Escobar was alone with a single bodyguard, Alvaro de Jesus Aguela, in a middle-class, two-story house in a Medellín *barrio*. Using the high-tech equipment supplied by the United States, Search Block intercepted a call Escobar made to his family, who were holed up in room 2908 of the *Residencias Tequendama* in Bogotá. Security personnel surrounded the house and cut the telephone lines in the *barrio* so no one could warn the drug lord.

Escobar never had a chance. On 2 December 1993, authorities knocked down the door and stormed the apartment. Dressed only in a T-shirt and jeans, Escobar fled to the roof, but his pursuers gunned him down. Autopsy reports later showed that he had been hit three times, with a shot to the head killing him instantly. Colombia breathed a sigh of relief. A Bogotá radio station reported the news of Escobar's death in mantra-like fashion, while in the background carolers sang "Joy to the World."

Ruiz Henao: "Escobar seemed invincible, and we never thought that the Colombian government would get him. I think the Colombian police murdered him. A few months later, I went to Medellín to visit Pablo Escobar's tomb. The people were still morning his death. Escobar was head of the Medellín Cartel, and his death reduced its power and influence."

In its hunt for Escobar, the US and Colombian governments had not totally ignored Cali. Even as the pursuit of Escobar intensified, authorities were working to penetrate Cali's infrastructure. They conducted a series of raids on drug processing labs, official residences, and offices belonging to the godfathers, destroying nearly twenty tons of processed cocaine and one hundred laboratories. In January 1992, the Colombian security forces conducted their first operation against the cartel's money-laundering operations, carrying out thirty-two simultaneous raids, not only in Cali but also in Bogotá and Barranquilla. They seized numerous computers, floppy disks, and twenty thousand other financial records, and uncovered information that led to three arrests and the freezing of fifteen million dollars in bank accounts in Colombia, Britain, Germany, Hong Kong, and the United States.

A third cartel, the *Norte del Valle* Cartel, the one Ruiz Henao was associated with directly, had not reached the level of power it would have in the drug trade in the late 1990s and early 2000s. Some of the leaders of the *Norte del Valle* Cartel came from Jesus' home town of Trujillo and one of the most powerful families within the Cali Cartel were the Henaos. The head of the family was Orlando Henao, *El Hombre del Overol* (the Overalls Man). He was considered richer and more powerful than Escobar, as he had many government officials, high-ranking military officers, and police on his payroll.

Ruiz Henao: "I have close family ties with many of the leaders of the *Norte del Valle* Cartel. Orlando Henao is my second-generation cousin, but we had never met or had done any business together due to a longstanding family feud between Orlando's grandfather, Gregory Henao, and my grandmother, Ana Henao. Don Diego Montoya Sanchez was a big boss and also came from Trujillo. It also happened that we had attended the same college in Trujillo called *La Concentration*."

In the mid-1980s, Montoya Sanchez ran cocaine laboratories that served many significant traffickers. By the late 1980s, Sanchez had expanded his organization's operations into smuggling plane loads of cocaine from Colombia to Mexico. In the early 1990s, he switched to maritime smuggling. During the course of the next fifteen years, Sanchez's organization routinely smuggled cocaine loads between one thousand and six thousand kilos at a time, using go-fast boats and fishing boats, among other methods.

At the time of Escobar's demise, the *Norte del Valle* Cartel was willing to defer to and work under the more powerful Cali Cartel. But after the collapse of Pablo Escobar's drug empire in 1993, the *Norte del Valle* often locked horns with the more powerful Cali Cartel. The aggression morphed into an all-out war following Cali Cartel leader Gilberto Rodríguez-Orejuela's announcement in 1995 that the Cali Cartel would be surrendering to the government in six months.

Ruiz Henao: "In early 1994, I attended many parties and festivals all over Colombia, visiting friends and making more contacts. I was introduced to a son of the general of the military police. We became very good friends and after several months, the son of the general told me that we can use one of the military planes to ship large quantities of cocaine from the jungle into the city. It was too big of an opportunity that I could not turn down.

"I bought some cocaine and had it delivered to a clandestine runaway in the Arauca region of Colombia. The next day, the cargo plane was loaded, and at 6 p.m., just before sunset, the huge plane taxied the runaway and took off. Then, as the plane reached approximately two hundred feet, it exploded right before our eyes. I, the general, his son, and few workers stood staring, unbelieving, and not knowing what to do as the enormous fiery wreckage plummeted to the ground. A few moments passed, and then we ran to the wreckage to see if anything was left. There was nothing, only pieces of metal and burning grass and trees. Everybody on board was killed. What wasn't burning was white from the cocaine powder.

"We panicked and ran back to our cars. We drove fast back to the city. I booked myself into a hotel and tried to stay calm. I did not phone anybody or tell anyone what had just happened. But one thing was for sure: once again, I was in debt. That cocaine load had cost me dearly. We never did find out what happened to the plane, but we think it was shot down by someone.

"Eventually, I went back to Pereira. I was nervous that someone was out to get me. I warned my wife, a strong, very loyal woman, to be aware that the next days would be very dangerous and difficult. She told me not to worry, that she would stand by my side. Pedro and Jose, my best friends, found out what had happened and offered to help.

"I moved my wife and small daughter to a rented two-bedroom house. I had no money. I had exhausted all of it to pay off debts. I was trying to sort out things when one night I received a beeper message from my wife telling me not to come home. There were armed *sicarios* waiting outside the house for me."

Sicarios are hired contract killers. They played a big role in the drug trade and helped to create the horrendous murder rate from the 1970s to the present day that has plagued Colombia. Many of the *sicarios* were poor and came from the slums of Medellin. They were recruited as teenagers and trained to be ruthless. Many were arrested or killed, but there was no shortage of new recruits to take their place.

"I was forced to spend the night somewhere else. The following day, I realized I had to confront the situation. I needed to do whatever was necessary to end it. But one night, my younger brother William went to a place to buy some marijuana. Some *sicarios* were getting high, and my brother managed to hear one of them saying, 'Tonight, we have to do him in, murder him.' They then mentioned my name.

"My brother jumped on his motorcycle and drove to my house. He told me what he had just heard. They were going to come for me tonight because I was very bad for their business. I took my wife and child and went to Armenia to stay with my friend Pedro. I told my neighbor to keep an eye on my place and to call me if someone came.

"My neighbor later told me that a car with four men was parked outside my home and that one of the men had knocked on my door. They were there until early in the morning. My friend Pedro gave me two grenades and a mini Uzi machine gun with a lot of ammunition. The next day,

I went back to my home well prepared and armed if they came back.

"I decided to go and see the leader of the *sicarios*, a man nicknamed Mico, to find out what was going on. I drove to his place in the west of Pereira. I parked my car close in case I needed to get away quickly. Mico was not there, and his workers were surprised to see me. They contacted Mico, and he arrived twenty minutes later. I explained to him my situation. He said that for the simple fact that I have the balls to show up personally meant that we could come to some kind of agreement. Don't worry, he assured me. We agreed to cooperate. I would have the time to pay my debt so long as I never tried to hide from him. I would have to answer the *sicarios'* calls any time they contacted me.

"By the end of 1994, I was well known for having good communication and negotiation skills, so the *sicarios* called me to help them. Because of my debts, I knew I could not refuse. But I was ambivalent. I wanted to make money in the drug business, not go around killing people.

"I was with the *sicarios* for a few months. They were getting paid to kill, and I was totally against that approach. Whenever I was involved in a negotiation for them, I would talk them out of using their guns. They became unhappy with me. They weren't getting paid because no one got murdered.

"One time, I travelled to Medellín with about ten heavily-armed *sicarios*. We arrived at around 7 a.m. and went into a corner coffee shop unaware there was a bank on the other corner. Within minutes, we were surrounded by more than forty well-armed police shouting to get on the ground. Because I was unarmed, I wasn't arrested, but all the *sicarios* were. I called my friend, the son of the military general, Tarazona Puyana, asking for his help. He said he would call me back. He did call and told me to go to the police station where the *sicarios* were held. I would sign some documents, bail papers. The officer in charge had been called by a high-ranking official from Bogotá, who told him that the *sicarios* were in fact security guards from one of his farms and were only going through the city. I went to the police station, signed the documents, and the *sicarios* were all released without delay. They were so happy. They became friendly with me and started to listen to my opinions.

"Later that day, we went to a block of apartments to see an old man, the father of an important person in the business. The *sicarios* demobilized the security men at the gate and entered the old man's apartment. I was waiting outside in the car and was told to come inside. The old man had locked himself in the toilet. The *sicarios* broke down the door and put the old man on to the floor. The old man made an attempt to grab the phone but was pushed into a corner.

"The *sicarios* wanted some information, but the old man insisted he did not have any. So the *sicarios* decided to murder him with a knife so as not to make any noise. The old man started to cry, saying that his son was a Colombian magistrate, somebody of importance, something of which I was totally unaware. The *sicarios* ignored the old man and were about to knife him when, on instinct, I jumped between the old man and the *sicarios*. We argued, but I convinced them, and the *sicarios* didn't kill the old man.

"The *sicarios*, however, were angry with me. They could have killed me, but they left. I told the old man not to worry. Nothing would happen to him. I walked out to the cars, but the *sicarios* were all gone. They were pissed and had left me without transport. So I had to walk to the bus station, where I caught a bus back to Pereira.

"After the five-hour bus ride, I arrived in Pereira. I went straight home to get the mini Uzi machine gun, then I went to the *sicarios'* office to confront them. I did not like being left stranded. When I arrived at their office, the gate was closed but I was allowed in. I concealed the machine gun under my coat. Mico, the leader, was there. He was surprisingly happy to see me. He didn't mention what had happened with the old man, but praised me for how I gotten all his men out of police custody. He said I had good contacts.

"I again called my friend, the son of the military general, asking him to put me in contact with the director of police for the city of Pereira. Mico had assured me that part of my debt would be paid off if I could get a meeting organized between him and the police director. When I spoke to the police director, he said he would be happy to meet with the *sicarios*. I told the *sicarios* leader and the date and time was set. Mico was extremely pleased.

"With the help of my friends Jose and Pedro, I managed to raise some money and went to Mico to pay off part of my debt. Mico refused to take the money and explained that my debt would be paid off once I helped him with another problem he had at the port of Buenaventura. They wanted me to get on one of the ships to make sure everything was okay with a drug shipment they were making. I was not happy, but I had no choice. If I was ever to be free of the debt, I would have to do as they asked.

"Weeks later, I travelled to the port of Buenaventura with several *sicarios*. The *sicarios* stayed in a house while I went to the port alone so as not to raise suspicions. I spoke to the port officer and told him that the ship could leave without delay, but I still needed to check the cargo.

"I rented a boat and hired three prostitutes to travel with me to the ship. We wanted to look like we were partying so as not to attract the attention of the marine police. When all looked well, I boarded the ship. The second-in-command was happy to take me to where the cocaine cargo was stored. I saw the cargo and took several photos of it. Then I spoke with the second-in-command. He informed me that they were a month behind and that the delivery would not be made for another three weeks. I left and went back to the port.

"I saw Mico and explained to him what the second-in-command had said. Mico became really angry. He said we needed to convince the port master to get the boat out on time. So we went to his house in an exclusive area of Buenaventura and knocked on his door. A huge, almost seven-foot-tall black man answered the door. Some of the *sicarios* went inside with me. We talked to the port master, but he said the boat could not leave earlier.

"The *sicarios* were angry. They decided the port master was of no further use to them, so they would kill him. They told me to leave. I started to walk out when suddenly the port master fell to his knees and started to pray. He implored: 'No, please; no, please.'

"I looked at him and he was sweating. His shirt was so soaked in sweat that it looked as though someone had poured a bucket of water over him. The man looked honest and surely didn't deserve to die. So I didn't leave. I told the *sicarios* to go and that I would deal with it. They grew very angry and swore at me. They threatened to kill me. One of them put his gun to my head. I told him: 'Do it and you'll have to explain to your boss what has happened because I'm taking responsibility.' The *sicarios* backed down.

"The port master realized how close he had come to dying. I explained to him that now it was not only his life in danger but mine as well. He promised me that that the delivery would be done before the three-week deadline. We went back to Pereira. The *sicarios* were angry with me again. They made it clear that I was solely and fully responsible if anything went wrong.

"When we stopped at a restaurant in the country to have lunch, the *sicario* in charge of our group came to me and said that the man who put his gun to my head would pay for it. I said: 'No, there's no problem.' Later that day, when we arrive to Pereira, I heard that the *sicarios* had murdered the *sicario* who had put the gun to my head.

"About two miles before we arrived at Pereira, we were met by the big boss's right-hand man. I was ordered into another car. We pulled away and later the right-hand man got into the car. I told him it was a real possibility that the cocaine would be delivered on time within three weeks. But he didn't believe me. I said that I wanted to speak to the big boss and explain it to him personally. He refused my request, but I insisted. He relented and said he would speak to the big boss. He would contact me in a few days with an answer.

"The big boss was my second-generation cousin, a man named Angel Henao, who lived in a town about a forty-minute drive from Pereira. My friend Don Pedro was a good friend of Angel Henao, and I was aware that he visited him at his villa regularly. Due to the long standing family feud, nobody knew of our family relation. It was something I kept quiet about. But now I needed to speak to him.

"I spoke with my friend Don Pedro, and he offered to drive me to see Angel Henao. When we arrived at the villa, I wasn't allowed inside, I had to stay outside, but as I was cleaning the car, I saw Angel Henao on the villa's football pitch. I never did get to speak to him. It was frustrating.

"Three weeks later, a group of men arrived at my home and told me that the right-hand man of Angel Henao wanted to see me. I was worried. It was three weeks and I had not heard if the drug shipment had arrived. But I went with them to a town called Cartago. I was taken to the villa of the Henao's right-hand man, who was in the garden drinking a beer. Upon seeing me, he rose and hugged me. He congratulated me. The shipment had arrived with no problems within the three-week deadline. I relaxed. My debt had finally been paid off. The *sicarios* knew they could trust me.

"I kept in constant contact with my two best friends, Jose and Pedro, getting our projects together and working to grow our drug business. A short while later, I was in Pereira when a friend drove by and picked me up. Soon after, a Toyota 4x4 pulled up behind us. Two men leaned out of the windows and began firing machine guns at us. My friend floored the car and drove as fast as he could to escape.

"I dropped to the floor, gun in hand, anxious. After a few minutes of driving like a maniac, we got away. When we were safe, my friend stopped the car, and we got out to look at the damage. The car was full of bullet holes and all the windows were shattered. It was a miracle we didn't get killed. After the incident, we asked around, but no one knew who was responsible.

"Weeks later, about two in the morning, I left a disco club located in an area of Pereira known as *La Badea*. I got into the car with my driver, and we made our way home. As we drove along the main road, we were suddenly blocked by two vehicles, one at the front and one at the back. The road we were on was very narrow. A steep hill went down to the river.

"I shouted to my driver to get off the road and move down the hill. Without hesitating, the driver did as he was told. We eventually crashed into a large rock. We got out and ran along the river, finally making it to a bridge. I got to a phone and called Jose to pick us up. My friends and I were very concerned because we had no idea who had attacked our vehicle.

"Clearly, my life was in danger. From whom, I didn't know. But I needed to do something quickly. I went to a friend who was very well respected by the *sicarios* in Pereira, a man nicknamed Tomaso. I told him what had been going on. He said he would conduct his intelligence to find out who was responsible. About a week later, Tomaso was in a corner coffee shop with his nephew having a coffee when suddenly two men appeared with machine guns and sprayed them with bullets, killing them both.

"I sent someone undercover to learn what happened. I found out who the killers were: Mico and his boys, the same men that I had stopped from killing the old man and the port master. I was told that they had decided to kill me because I stopped them from murdering the two men. Not killing the two men had cost them money. I had to go.

"I immediately contacted the right-hand man of my cousin Angel Henao and told him what had happened. He said to be extremely careful over the next few days while he would set up a meeting with them. Days later, the meeting was held in a car sales shop in Pereira where the *sicarios* had their main office. I was told to be there. They were all in the main office's lounge area, including Mico.

"My cousin's right-hand man put his hand on my shoulder and told them: 'This man here is my friend, and all of you must respect him. From now on, there will be no mercy to anyone who attacks him.' He then told them to leave. After they left, he told me that even though they had been warned, I should remain alert, careful, and vigilant. He recommended I leave the country. My life was in serious danger."

By now, the Colombian drug trade had changed dramatically. After Escobar was killed in 1993, the Cali Cartel became drug enforcement's number-one target. It had a global reach and thousands of employees and was involved in every aspect of the drug trade. It had forged alliances with Italian, Russian, Mexican, British, Japanese, and other drug traffickers, helping to spawn the emergence of transnational crime as a major threat to the global community.

And so at the height of its power in the early 1990s, the Cali Cartel was running its criminal empire more on the model of a multinational corporation than a criminal enterprise. It treated its members like company employees, hired the best person for the job, used business strategy to market its illegal product, and shifted operations from one locale to another as economic and political conditions necessitated.

The godfathers from the Cali Cartel did not kill leading citizens of the state as the Medellín Cartel did, nor engage in narco terrorism. So for nearly two decades, the Colombian government and its US ally focused on Escobar and the Medellín Cartel, a strategy that allowed the Cali Cartel the space to grow its criminal enterprise. Consequently, the cartel was able to dominate the cocaine market by the early 1990s.

The Cali Cartel's low-key style helped it build extensive distribution networks right under the noses of international law enforcement, giving the cartel an initial advantage against its adversary. Even when law enforcement discovered the cartel's existence in the mid-1980s and what it was doing within their communities, it was extremely difficult for the authorities to penetrate and disrupt it. The cartel operated with the compartmentalization of a terrorist organization, while its associates were willing to go to jail, fearing what could happen to them and their families if they informed. Besides, they knew that the cartel would take care of their families while they were in jail.

The downfall of the Cali Cartel was in many ways a creation of its own success. Like any well-run multinational corporation, the cartel kept meticulous records of its business activities, including personnel matters. New employees were required to fill out application forms. Employees got holidays and were paid bonuses. This paper trail would assist law enforcement in tracking the cartel's operations.

Authorities began to discern the smuggling routes and began making arrests in Colombia, the United States, Latin America, and Europe. With the arrests, the cartel's cell structure began to break down, and some of those arrested—despite their well-placed fear—began to become informants.

As law enforcement successfully investigated the cartel's operations, the cartel found it increasingly difficult to hire the talent it needed to fill the ranks of its depleted managerial pool. It didn't help the cartel either that the wrong "CEO" was running affairs at the most critical juncture in its development. Miguel Rodríguez-Orejuela, who took over the cartel's day-to-day management about 1990, was a micro-manager who couldn't seem to let go of business matters or delegate responsibility.

Micro-managing affairs in the United States and Europe from headquarters in Cali could work early in its history when the cartel was small and law enforcement had little inkling about its activities, but not when it became the size of IBM or General Motors. In fact, Miguel's micro-managing style became a liability. Imagine the CEO of IBM or General Motors, based in New York City, directly trying to oversee business operations in its chief market, Colombia. Sooner or later, communication is bound to break down.

By 1995, the Colombian government assigned five hundred soldiers and police to a unit known as Search Block, with the sole responsibility of tracking and taking down the Rodríguez-Orejuela brothers and their key subordinates. The government also announced a reward of $1.6 million. Between June and July 1995, six of the seven remaining heads of the Cali Cartel were arrested. Gilberto was arrested in his home. Miguel was captured after a betrayal by Jorge Salcedo, the Cali Cartel's head of security.

Colombian law forbids extradition of any prisoners for crimes committed before 16 December 1997. The brothers were safe from being extradited to the United States, but the opportunity to become the new kings of Colombian had been opened for Jesus Ruiz Henao and the *Norte del Valle* Cartel.

According to Pete Walsh, the fall of the Medellín and Cali leadership had little or no impact on the cocaine trade to the UK and Europe. "Both the Medellín and Cali Cartels were loose alliances of numerous smaller or less infamous trafficking groups, and the removal of the very top tier – Escobar, the Rodríguez-Orejuelas, Pacho Herrera, etc. – which the US defined as its 'Kingpin Strategy,' had no discernible impact on those other smuggling groups, which simply continued about their business. In many cases, they actually expanded: the North Valley Cartel, for example.

The ultimate drivers of the trade – supply and demand – were simply unstoppable at that stage."

FOUR

BACK IN THE UNITED KINGDOM

Jesus thought it best to take the advice to leave Colombia for the sake of both his family and himself. "I didn't like the violence in Colombia. If I would have stayed I would have had to start using a gun. In all likelihood I would have been dead. There is no way around it. The only way I could avoid the violence was to leave the country."

In November 1995, he left Colombia, travelling to Madrid with his wife and daughter.

"While I was in Madrid, I contacted some of my Italian friends in Barcelona and made some more friends. Early 1996, I moved to Paris, France, and explored the possibility of setting up a business, but I couldn't work anything out. So I moved to London, back to where I knew there was a very good market for cocaine."

It was a very good time to move into the trade. The main reason for this had little to do with cocaine itself.

Pete Walsh: "In the late 1980s, British youth were gripped by the acid house scene. A new kind of repetitive dance music overtook the country's nightclubs. With it came unprecedented levels of usage of a manufactured recreational stimulant, ecstasy, which was ideally suited to the experience of house music. From total obscurity, ecstasy became the drug of choice for vast swathes of British youth within the space of just a few years.

"Once such a large number of normally law-abiding young people had come to accept consumption of an illegal drug as part of their normal weekend activities, it was a short step to acceptance of another illicit stimulant—cocaine—which had its own alluring properties.

"In a way, ecstasy 'softened up' the market for coke, making it more acceptable. Coupled with a surge in cocaine supply to Europe as the US market began to reach saturation, this meant that by the late 1990s, cocaine was the drug in the United Kingdom."

By then, the British cocaine market had changed dramatically since the mid-1980s.

"It was around 1983 that British law enforcement first spotted a marked rise in cocaine importation. Between 1982 and 1983, the total annual amount seized by HM Customs and Excise (HMCE) rose six fold, and in 1984, HMCE's Investigation Division formed a special team to investigate cocaine trafficking for the first time. It quickly took off, and soon several teams were assigned to cocaine."

Once you start looking, you tend to find. Within a short time, they were turning up significant cases. Interestingly, they found that Bolivians, rather than Colombians, were targeting the UK market.

Walsh: "The Colombians then were preoccupied with the USA, where the market was nearer and bigger and where they were making easy fortunes. British investigators and politicians travelled to Bolivia to learn more about what was going on there, and the Investigation Division began a program of placing anti-drug officers overseas in certain key countries, something the DEA had been doing for decades, but which was new for the Brits.

"But it didn't take long for the Colombian cartels to expand into Europe. In 1985, the DEA's chief in Bogotá visited London to brief British law enforcement and warn them that Colombians were already operating there. The DEA even passed on some names.

"The problem both the Bolivians and the Colombians had, at that stage, was finding British wholesalers willing to buy from them in bulk. The big producers were not interested in selling just a few kilos. But the UK cocaine market was still so immature that it was hard to move the kinds of amounts that might typically sell in a US city. The South Americans did not understand this and became very suspicious when Brits took a delivery of drugs from them and then did not pay promptly. They thought they were being ripped off. In fact, the Brits were struggling to sell it and to raise the cash to pay them back.

"The first sign that the market had expanded sufficiently to warrant major importations came in July 1986, and involved a number of notorious figures from the London underworld. They managed to make a link to the infamous Ochoa family through a connection in Miami, and arranged a smuggling operation by private boat of 392 kilos. No such amount had ever been heard of in the UK before. The smuggle was successful, but the gang was captured after selling only some of the coke, and received long jail terms. This was a wake-up call for law enforcement.

"From then on the market continued to grow and grow. Interestingly, however, the UK generally avoided the plague of crack cocaine that devastated many US inner cities. This was perhaps because it was not possible to manufacture and sell crack to the masses as cheaply as it was in the US. The transport costs alone, across the Atlantic Ocean, meant cocaine was always dearer in the UK."

Ruiz Henao: "I rented an apartment in the Holloway Road area and contacted some people who had been recommended to me. One of them was a man named Tito. I was told he was a hard worker and could be trusted.

"Tito became one of my daily contacts in the cocaine business. He was aware of all the stash sites, delivery addresses, and quantities I had. Tito introduced me to Beto, his cousin, who became another trusted colleague. He would rent the stash addresses using a Spanish passport.

"We worked out a plan. The drugs and money would always be stashed separate, never together. If an address was ever compromised, that is, seized, one or the other would be lost, but not both. Whenever our men visited any of the stash sites we had placed in Tottenham, Russell Square, Swiss Cottage, and Camden Town, they would always carry books in hold-alls to look like students. Actually, that was done before the 9/11 terrorist incident. After 9/11 it was impossible to carry a hold-all.

"At this stage, the operation needed to stay small with just a couple of people and two cars. One of my golden rules was not to have any contact with people involved in my cocaine business once an agreement had been reached.

"I remember my first deal. I met the person in a gym. As soon as he found out I was Colombian, he started pestering me for drugs. Two or three weeks later, I made a deal. I sold him half a kilo and made twenty thousand pounds. I sent a man to complete the deal. I never dealt directly with him. I did some other deals with him, but the man talked too much. He bragged he had a Colombian connection. The police eventually arrested him.

"In October 1996, I received a message from a Spanish contact requesting we meet at the Warren Street McDonald's in two hours. I called Tito and together we went to the meeting. The Spaniard was already there and told me that he had a gift for me. Tito went with him to an underground car park where he was given some clothes and two kilo blocks of cocaine in a plastic bag. Tito immediately took the cocaine to the Tottenham stash apartment and secured it there.

"Because my English language wasn't good at this stage and a single word can change the meaning of a subject, it was important that everything I said had to be clear, with no confusion. I called my brother-in-law Mario Tascon, who speaks very good English, and asked him to help me with the language and to make sure that everything said was completely understood.

"At first he didn't really want to come in. But he became like my right-hand man in the drug business. He would handle things when I was away. I would take him to meetings, and he would help with the translation. Because of his language help, he became totally aware of everything in my organization. That's all. I know the press described him as my partner, but he was just somebody who worked for me. Unfortunately, he was arrested the same day as I was and was sentenced to seventeen years in prison for conspiracy to traffic in drugs.

"The day after I hired Mario, I went with him to see a British friend, a builder, at his construction site. I told him that I had some 'charlie,' or cocaine, for sale. The builder said his brother-in-law would be interested in buying a kilogram. He told me to go to his house in the Hammersmith area Saturday evening.

"On that Saturday, during the day, I went to see an Ecuadorian girl called Elsy who I knew. Elsy was very sharp, and I came to work with her closely. I had already explained to her the business and offered her a pay deal that she accepted. I took her to the stash address, parked my car around the corner and left her in the car. I went to Tito at the stash house and picked up a kilogram of cocaine. I went back to the car where I gave Elsy the kilo. She put it in her handbag.

"I then drove to the Hammersmith area to see the builder. We sat in his living room waiting for the brother-in-law to arrive. An half an hour later, the brother-in-law came. We got the cocaine and went to the kitchen to test the purity. It was eighty-seven percent pure, of good quality. He wanted the whole kilo but couldn't pay for the whole. He needed three days to get the money. I thought about it. This wasn't a good situation. It involved risk. But I knew to start the business, I had to take risks. Besides, I was aware where he and his family lived, and he knew it. That to me was pretty much of a guarantee that he would pay. So I gave him the kilo.

"The next day, I contacted another English friend I had met a year before and offered him cocaine. The man readily agreed to buy some, but he was unemployed and had no collateral. He needed credit for a quarter of a kilo. He would pay for it the next day, he promised me. Again, it was another risk. But I was building a business and risk was part of it, so I agreed.

"I introduced him to Elsy, my Ecuadorian associate, and explained that she would be his contact from now on. I went to my stash of cocaine and cut the other kilo in four equal pieces, wrapping them in a silk paper. I took a quarter and gave it to Elsy. I drove her to an underground station, and she went off to sell it.

"After just a few hours, the man called and said he needed another quarter. So I took the remaining three-quarters and handed it to Elsy. I instructed her to take the money for the first quarter, telling her to tell him that it was safer to do fewer deliveries and for him to pay for every quarter he bought. The man was very happy that I had trusted him. Still, it was a big risk. Five days later, I had the entire money from both buyers. For me, the risk had paid off.

"I had remarkably good luck in getting the money; I only lost a drug load two times. It was two kilos when I first started, and later when I was trafficking huge loads, I lost fourteen kilos. At the time of my arrest, about eighty kilos were intercepted. That was it. Truly amazing. I know the DEA admits it only intercepts fifteen percent of the drugs being trafficked. I think that figure is a lot lower in the UK.

"Once we delivered the shipment, the connection in Colombia wanted his money quickly. They did not like to wait for it. We had counting machines and we packed the money in bundles, five thousand or ten thousand pounds per bundle. We had no problem with theft. I would bundle fourteen thousand pounds and tell my workers there were £110,000, and they would tell me the correct amount. They knew there were big time, dangerous people behind me who would kill in a heartbeat. Or at least that is what I made them think.

"Now I needed to send some of the money back to Colombia. I bought a suitcase and opened the bottom of it. I put the money, about the forty thousand pounds in five thousand pound bundles, and handed the suitcase to a Spanish man, who came to pick it up. I had made a fantastic profit.

"I brought another trusted worker to the United Kingdom from Colombia with whom to work. His nickname was Tito, and he became my right-hand man. I bought a new car for Tito.

"I was careful to distance myself from my associates. I would only deal with the money. Everything ran smoothly. The Spaniard would contact Tito, and he and Elsy would deliver the cocaine to the contacts. When the money was ready, I would go and collect it.

"I was still not making enough money from cocaine trafficking, so I had to work at a regular job. I took a job as a bus driver. I liked the job. I was out and about and the job paid well. I never experienced discrimination because I was a Colombian immigrant. I was treated well. But my cocaine business was starting to pay off. I was finding it very easy to get the cocaine into the United Kingdom. So I had to make a decision. The cocaine trade in the United Kingdom was booming. I quit my bus driving job and delved into the cocaine trade full time.

"I had a lot to learn as a drug trafficker. The fact is you learn something every single day. It's like anything. You learn by experience, but in the drug trade, learning can be dangerous. You can say you will learn from your mistakes, but one mistake can land you in jail, or, worse, get you killed. You have to stay one step in front of the authorities and the gangsters, which is not easy. You make one mistake with the police and you die or end up in prison. You make one mistake with your fellow gangsters and you die, period.

"I did have a close call, in 1996, in the United Kingdom. I was actually arrested. I was carrying a couple of grams of cocaine. The police didn't know I was a dealer, so they let me go. I really didn't have a close call again until the end when I came under police investigation.

"I was the one who opened the UK market for Colombian cocaine. In 1995 or 1996, it was a very small market, just a few kilos for a deal. I started in 1994 and by 1996, dealing for me had become real big. The English authorities were not ready for me. They didn't do proper intelligence. They relied on technology. They didn't spend too much time cultivating human intelligence or informants. It was not like the American or Colombian police, who do proper intelligence. They don't sit in the office waiting for someone to tell them what's going on.

"My greatest strength, I think, was my ability to deal with people, to negotiate a deal, get people to do what I wanted them to do. I was a good communicator. I have the power to explain things to people and get things done. In what I said, there was an implication. I would tell them I was just a messenger. I work for people in Colombia who are really powerful. If you don't want to do something, you will have to answer to them. I was playing a game, but I was convincing.

"My associates in the drug trade knew I would always keep my word. People trusted me, and I could get them to do what I wanted. If I told someone that I needed the million pounds by 1 p.m., I would have it by 1 p.m. That kind of trust in the drug trade is uncommon. People will lie to you, try to cheat you. They think they have to screw you before you screw them. I didn't operate that way. You don't need to operate that way. Look at the success I had as a drug kingpin!"

In December 1996, Jesus was contacted by a boss from Pereira, Colombia, via his friend Pedro. He was given a number, a code, to pick up some money for him in London. Jesus decoded the number and got a password.

Ruiz Henao: "From a brand new mobile number, I contacted the person the boss had told me to contact. When the person answered, I said the password and was told to meet at 1 p.m. that Saturday in a pub near the Hampstead underground station. Another of my golden rules was that whenever I had to be at a meeting, I would always be early. I did this so I could get familiar with the place and surroundings. It would give me a chance to take a good look around and get a sense if there was anything wrong. I trusted my gut feeling.

"So that Saturday, I arrived about midday and started walking around, checking everything and looking everywhere. Things seem normal. About an hour later, I noticed two men, one young and one old, chatting. They glanced at me.

"As I got near them, they instinctively said hello. The older man was very well dressed in a white shirt and jacket and had a walking stick. He was about sixty-five years old and spoke with an accent. He extended his right hand to me, then said the password. He put his hand into his jacket pocket, took out some car keys and handed them to me. He gave me the car registration number, make and model, and told me it was parked around the corner. The money was in the trunk.

"I asked the older man what I had to do with the car once I had removed the money. 'Nothing,' the man replied. 'The car is yours too.' I drove the car to the stash flat in Russell Square and parked it in the car park. There, I looked into the car trunk and inside were some black bin bags full of cash. I was shocked! I was thinking there would be around one hundred thousand pounds to collect, but I was looking at much, much more.

"I contacted the man in Colombia who owned the money to find out what he wanted me to do with so much cash. The boss wasn't in a hurry. He told me to count it, keep it in a safe place, and start sending it over slowly. A large portion of that money was for me. I moved all the money from the car to the flat. I unpacked the black bags and stocked the money on the other side in the room. I looked at all the cash piled up. Never had I seen so much cash together.

"I disconnected all the telephonic devices, including the television, locked the door, and grabbed a notebook and a pen. I sat in a chair and stared at the money, hundreds of bundles of all kinds of bills, in various denominations. I counted late into the afternoon with no idea when I would finish. I counted all through the night, putting together ten, twenty, and fifty thousand-pound bundles, all tied in elastic bands.

"By early morning, I had counted more than two million pounds, but I still had a lot left to count. I needed a rest, so at 9 a.m., I took public transport home. I had a shower and went to bed. At 2 p.m., I went to pick up the Ecuadorian girl Elsy so she could help me count the money. With Elsie's help, we finished counting the money late that night. I was tired, but I was jacked up by being surrounded by millions of pounds. We partied in the flat for the remainder of the night.

"It was a week before Christmas. I would have no contact with the boss until January or February. At this time of the year, they stopped all communication related to business and did not work. They spent time with their families.

"At the end of January 1997, I managed to make contact with the owner of the money. To my surprise, he didn't ask how much money there was; in fact, no one had asked me that question. And no one told me how much there should be. I was simply told to send the money to Colombia by *giros*, or money transfers, bit by bit, and not to worry, to take my time. It would take forever, since, if I sent the money by *giros* as the max allowed by law, I could only send five hundred pounds per customer.

"Dealing with the money was a real hassle. I think it's the toughest part of being a drug dealer. If you are really successful, you have so much money to handle. The drugs come in, you handle it, and they go out. The money hangs around. You're dealing with millions. You can always dump the money in a stash house, but you are always worrying that somebody will find it. You ask yourself: 'How the hell can I deal with it?'

"You can minimize the number of people who know about the stash house. You put somebody in the stash house to guard it twenty-four hours a day. There is a telephone but no television in the stash house. The guard can't leave the stash house. He's paid well. I paid my guards up to a thousand pounds a day. A stash house would hold from two to five million pounds. One stash house I had contained thirty thousand pounds. A lot of money, a lot of temptation, but with regard to my stash houses, I did everything right. No one ever betrayed me. But I was still up at night worrying.

"In Southeast London, near Kensington Underground Station at Braganza Street, was a *giro* company. The director told me to drop between fifty to one hundred thousand pounds per week, but even with this, it would take months because of the phenomenal amount of money I was holding. I had to send a ton of money overseas, so I realized I needed to start thinking about different, better ways to launder money.

"From this moment, I became known as one of the most successful money launderers in the drug business. I made a fortune using more and more sophisticated methods to launder huge sums of money. At my sentencing, the word 'sophisticated' was used on several occasions by the judge with respect to the sheer quantity of money I laundered.

"By mid-February 1997, I had managed to send over five hundred thousand pounds to Colombia. I contacted my friend Jose, who happened to be with the owner of the money. It was then that I was asked for the first time how much money I had received. I calculated it to be about £7.2 million. I knew I was being tested because I had been told by a nephew in Colombia that they were expecting me to tell them a different sum of money. I knew, however, that to earn their trust and to survive in the drugs business, I had to be truthful or I wouldn't last very long at all.

"Two months later, I was contacted again by the owner of the money. By this time, I had already sent £6.4 million to Colombia. He told me everything was good and that he had the money. Keep the rest for me as my profit. That was great. For sending money to Colombia, I got more than eight hundred thousand pounds in profit. I split this profit with some of the boys who were with me at that time. I always gave Tito a bit more than the others because he was the one closest to me. Besides, he was one of my direct contacts, and through him, I gave orders to my men about what they had to do during the day.

"Several weeks later, I was contacted by someone in London who said he was the brother-in-law of the owner of the money. He said he needed to speak to me. Meet me by the Leicester Square area at a pub that day, he instructed. As usual, I called the girl Elsy to be my company, and we went and met the man. He was there waiting for me with two Spaniards. He asked me to pick up some money (*pesetas*) and to get a car ready for them for tomorrow. They said they would give the car back to me in the evening. It would be loaded with cocaine.

"I did as they said. I sent Tito to collect the money: one million Spanish *pesetas*, which, at the time, was about five hundred thousand pounds. I packed the Spanish money in different sized parcels and stored them in a fridge like frozen food.

"That evening, Tito and I were waiting for the car to be given back to us. I arranged for the car to be driven to Finsbury Park Station and to the mini cab station that was open twenty-four hours a day. I went to play pool around the corner. At about 2 a.m., the car arrived, driven by one of the Spaniards. He got out the car and went to the mini cab office to have a coffee. About five minutes later, I entered the mini cab office and ordered two coffees for Tito and myself. We picked up the coffees and went to a table close to the Spaniard. He saw us and finished his coffee without saying a word. He went out into the streets and walked away.

"Tito and I finished our coffee, and because we had a second set of the car keys, I told Tito to drive the car around to the next corner. As he drove around, I had a quick glimpse inside the car. I clearly saw a couple of kilos of cocaine in the backseat. I told Tito to cover them with his jacket and to drive really carefully to our main Tottenham stash house.

"The next morning, I communicated with Tito, and he told me that there were one hundred kilos. I told him to deliver ten kilos to the builder at Hammersmith and ten to another contact that I had made, whom we called *La Paloma* (the Dove). The quality of the drugs was super, flakey and crystal. Two contacts came to us and asked if they could buy the entire load. I split the eighty kilos left between them, and three days later, I received all the money for this sale, about £2.3 million.

"I waited to hand over the money. About a week later, I was contacted by them. I told them to meet Tito, who will give them the money. I heard that one of them was arrested in Spain, but they wanted to continue working with me. Because of this situation, I decided to travel to Colombia to speak to Jose and to the big boss about it. More importantly, I wanted to get permission to work with the Spaniards.

"In December 1997, I flew to Colombia to see my two friends, Pedro and Jose. I stayed in one of their villas. I explained to them the reason why I traveled to Colombia.

They backed my decision to start working with the Spaniards. A few days later, we went to see the big boss at his villa. There were many bodyguards. The big boss didn't come out to speak to us. He just sent a messenger to tell us everything was good and that he was giving us the green light to work with the Spaniards.

"I mentioned the Spanish money that I had frozen in London. Minutes later, the big boss called me to the sitting room where he was. He asked me how much money there was, and I told him around fifty thousand pounds. He said: 'Okay, I'll tell you what to do.' But when I told him that the money was in old Spanish currency, *pesetas*, he told me: 'Keep it. Let's have a drink to that.' He was friendly and gave me the confidence to ask about the Spaniards and if it was okay for me to work with them. He shook my hand and said: 'Boy, you are doing the right thing. Do as you wish.' I now had the authority to begin my dream of making a lot of money.

"In early 1998, I went to the Fulham Broadway Underground to meet a group of Argentinians who needed distribution in the UK. The Argentinians were recommended to me by my friend Pedro in Colombia. I have never met a new contact on my own. This time I contracted with an escort girl to go with me.

"We met in the Blue Elephant restaurant, near Chelsea. When we arrived, there were a lot of formalities, and we talked about different things. Eventually, we got down to business. They had a large shipment of drugs arriving into the UK in a matter of days, and they needed me to deal with the distribution and to organize sending the money back to Colombia.

"Three weeks later, I was contacted by an Argentinian woman named Maria Linares. She told me to meet her in a restaurant near Hammersmith Palace and that she needed to explain something to me. I sent Tito with the Ecuadorian girl, Elsy, on my behalf. Tito reported back to me that the meeting with the Argentinian woman had gone okay. So, later that day, I arranged to meet her in a pub.

"Maria Linares explained to me that she needed to supply a Italian-English man known as *La Paloma* (the Dove) and said that the drug shipment they had been waiting for had been lost somewhere in mainland Europe before it could arrive in the UK. Her Argentinian associates had already flown back to South America. I told Tito and Beto to start working with her, but to only start with five kilos at the time. Maria Linares was extremely effective in collecting the money and making payments. So soon we started to supply her with fifty to one hundred kilos at a time. Many times when I received a shipment from Colombia, Maria would take all of it to *La Paloma.*

"After nearly two years of doing business with Maria Linares, I went with Tito to meet her in a coffee shop near Baker Street. She wanted to open another cocaine distribution route. To Maria, I was known as Lucas. Very few people knew me by my real name. They would call me Lucas, which in Colombian Spanish slang means *money.* That seemed perfect since many people I knew would tell me that I could turn 'shit' (cocaine) into money.

"Maria told me that she needed more cocaine from us to start another distribution route. Half an hour later, she met with my man Beto near the West Hampstead Underground Station. Beto gave Maria the ten kilos she needed to start her new distribution route. Beto was instructed to follow her. When they parted, Beto stayed back and watched her walk to her car.

"Maria got into her car and started the engine. But soon the police came out of the woodwork and arrested her. Beto saw everything. He ran away from the scene and was not followed. He managed to get a message to Tito, who, in turn, informed me about what had happened.

"I froze with fear. I had been sharing a coffee with her no more than an hour before. Was she being followed the whole time? Were the police after me now? There was also a big problem because Maria Linares, as the middle woman between me and *La Paloma*, had taken a delivery of one hundred kilos to *La Paloma* the day before. Now, with her arrest, Maria had no way of contacting him for the payment.

"It seemed at this point that the police hadn't followed Maria or seen our meeting. So I thought I was safe for now. I contacted Maria's husband and told him I needed to see *La Paloma*. The husband agreed to arrange a meeting.

"Initially, both of us sent a worker to establish contact and break the ice. The first meeting took place in a McDonald's in South Wimbledon. After a couple of meetings, *La Paloma* supplied the money for a one hundred-kilo shipment (2.7 million pounds), and asked that the business arrangements Maria had with me be reestablished.

"Days later, I met *La Paloma* personally and found out that he was called Danny. The business grew considerably and continued for nearly two years until Danny, or *La Paloma*, was arrested. This cost me two million pounds. After I was arrested in 2003, I found out that Maria Linares was set up by the new contact she was trying to do business with, an undercover policeman.

"By this time, I was making a lot of money. I became interested in Mozambique. The people there were very poor. It was Christmas and I could see they had no presents, so I bought them some. I thought to myself: if there are poor people in England like her, what about in Colombia, which was a poor country? How many children were there, who needed help and who were hungry?

"I said to myself: 'You're making all this money. Come on, help them out.' So I made a decision to help the children. That's when I started an orphanage. It is located in a village close to Pereira. The children from the orphanage have grown up. Some of the children now are in their early thirties.

"I actually help a lot of children, especially those in Mozambique and Honduras. I did charity for a Catholic priest, and I would send money through him to Mozambique. It was maybe about ten thousand pounds. I also helped children through the World Vision Foundation. It made me feel really good."

FIVE

TRAFFICKING IN SUBURBIA

In March 2001, Jesus Ruiz Henao settled in Hendon, a very nice and quiet middle-class neighborhood in the London suburbs, population about 53,000. Jesus bought a large house that was built in the 1930s, and he contracted a company to refurbish it. He enlarged the rooms and built pillars in the Italian style. It was like a palace inside, but on the outside, he conserved the original design of the building.

Ruiz Henao: "I really liked the neighborhood. It had a lot of privacy, and people stayed out of each other's business. It was so easy to notice anything out of the ordinary. When the police had me under surveillance, I could see them going to my neighbor, and I knew the police were on to me.

"The neighbors were pleasant but cold. I lived in the neighborhood for nearly a decade and didn't get to know anyone. The English are not like the Spanish, who are very friendly and want to get to know you. I remember when one person died in the neighborhood, and the body was discovered about a month later only because of the smell.

"Three doors down the road, I bought a similar house for my security to live in. They were armed and fully alert for any action if trouble brewed. That included the police. I had vowed to my associates in Colombia that I would never go to prison or surrender alive.

"Luckily, or maybe the police were aware of my intentions, they arrested me before I had a chance to act. When the British police found out about the house, they were surprised and questioned me on several occasions. They peppered me with questions: Why that house? What was I planning?

"A few months after my arrest, my security, which consisted of three Colombians and two Italians, were arrested in a garage in South London. They were each sentenced to eight years in prison for firearms offenses. They were incarcerated in the same prison as me, in Belmarsh high-security prison. I was never allowed to get close to them, not even during the Sunday Catholic services. If they went, I wasn't allowed to go, and if I went, they weren't allowed.

"When I moved to Hendon, I was making a lot of money, but I was still working a regular job as a bus driver. I knew I had to be disciplined and keep a low profile. Who would imagine a budding drug lord driving a bus or cleaning offices or working in an Italian coffee shop?

"I lived a normal life, went to a normal job, and drove a normal car. I had seen what happened to Escobar, Lehder, and the leaders of the Cali Cartel. They got too big for their pants. I kept a low profile. None of my family knew about my drug trafficking. I would kiss my wife goodbye each day and go to work. She suspected nothing. I liked working, but I had to quit my job because I was constantly making drug deals on the job, and it became too much.

"I never talked to anybody about my drug tracking activities. I was just your normal immigrant trying to build a better life for himself and his family in a new country. Whenever I made a deal, I would tell the buyer I was just a messenger working for somebody. They never fathomed that I was the real Mr. Big.

"I never kept large quantities of money in the house. I tried to act like your average citizen. I would make monthly payments on my mortgage every month. I would buy furniture on credit.

"I always kept the money in safe houses. I had about five of them, three with money and two with drugs. I always kept the drugs and the money separate. It was just a preference of mine. If a safe house is busted, you lose either the drugs or money, not both. I always felt that when you keep money and drugs together something will invariably go wrong. I did it once and lost more than two million pounds and one hundred kilos of cocaine. The police had stopped one of my men, and he talked.

"I was always worried about informants like the snitch who did something stupid and drew attention to himself. So my drug organization had a golden rule: if I found out someone was flashing money, I would kick him out of the organization. Fortunately, that happened only once. I would go to the chapel every Sunday. One of my close friends came up to me and said: 'Listen. I heard one of your men was at a seaside resort in the summertime spending a lot of money, about ten thousand to twenty thousand pounds, and driving a very flashy car. He is raising suspicions.'

"I contacted him and set up a meeting. He tried to deny it, but I said: 'Listen, Carlos, don't be stupid. I know what you did. I have witnesses.' I wasn't afraid he would turn on me. He was a low-level associate who just ran one of my stash houses. He had limited knowledge of my organization. He really could not tell the authorities anything. Besides, I closed down that stash house and moved the money from it to another one."

In 1998, Ruiz Henao began doing drug business with Spaniards. Spain had become an important conduit for international drug trafficking. In the late 1970s and early 1980s, the main Colombian cartels, particularly the Cali Cartel, saw that Europe was a great market for them, and they wanted to find a gateway. The US market for cocaine was starting to become saturated by the mid-1980s. The street price had dropped nearly two-thirds, while cocaine was selling for four times as much in Europe.

The Cali Cartel recognized that the European drug market was ripe for penetration. When Jorge Ochoa from the Medellín Cartel and Miguel Rodríguez-Orejuela, Cali Cartel's leader, moved to Spain in 1984, they bought a large ranch in Badajoz, near the border with Portugal. It would serve as a base of operations from which they could analyze the potential for trafficking cocaine in Europe. They found in Galicia, Spain, a corner of Europe with an open coastline, controlled by smuggler clans who enjoyed social support and were not bothered by local politicians.

The Cali Cartel reached out to the tobacco smugglers from Galicia, who had a good knowledge of the region's coastline and storage facilities that could be used to smuggle drugs. The cartel began using boats to pick up the drugs from ocean-going vessels and bring them ashore. To launder its money, it set up a network of accounts between Spanish and Panamanian banks and invested in real estate.

Jorge Ochoa sent one of his key lieutenants, Teodoro Castrillon, to England, Germany, and Holland to establish contacts with the local Colombian communities and to see if they could develop the infrastructure and distribution networks similar to those they had in the United States. Gilberto and Jorge and their wives, however, were arrested near Rodríguez-Orejuela's apartment in Madrid. Rodríguez-Orejuela and Ochoa were deported to Colombia, where they were released and avoided prison.

The Colombians, however, had established a foothold in Spain from which to move into the rest of Europe. The United Kingdom became an important potential market. It had seen an explosion in heroin consumption from the late 1970s onwards, but didn't as yet have a significant coke problem. In 1985, a female cousin of the Ochoas opened up a supply line with her English husband, Keith Goldsworthy, a pilot. Goldsworthy would fly hundreds of kilos into the US in his private Cessna and then ship it to England. A parallel supply route was opened up by Fabio Ochoa personally on a visit to London.

Within a year, cocaine seizures in the UK had doubled. Goldsworthy was eventually caught in Miami and jailed for twenty-two years, but by then, the genie was out of the bottle. Four years after the arrival of Rodríguez-Orejuela and Ochoa in Spain, the Cali Cartel had made significant inroads in a drug market long dominated by heroin. Surveys conducted in the countries of the European community verified these observations. In the European community, cocaine seizures skyrocketed from nine hundred kilograms in 1985 to thirteen tons in 1990. Three years later, the cartel had so refined the European smuggling network that they were using many of the major commercial ports in Europe, including Liverpool, Hamburg, Genoa, and Rotterdam.

Ruiz Henao: "The Spaniards would arrive from Spain about once a month with from eighty to three hundred kilograms of cocaine. Once in the UK, the cocaine was taken to safe houses, mostly in North London, where it was reconstituted and packaged for distribution throughout the country. Many of those on my UK end of the operation were relatives, or close family friends back in Colombia. The drugs were sold to British crime groups, who, in turn, sold it on the streets."

Getting the profits back to Colombia was also well organized. Sometimes the smugglers simply filled hold-alls with cash and popped them back on the lorries that had brought the drugs. Alternatively, couriers would swallow condoms full of rolled-up one hundred pound notes.

"When a new lorry arrived, I would give them all the money from the previous cocaine shipment. They paid in British pounds and the Spanish *peseta* (the Euro wasn't in circulation at the time). Months later, I was introduced to someone who had connections with one of the most powerful organizations in the UK, the Freemasons."

Freemasonry is one of the world's oldest social and charitable organizations. Its roots lie in the traditions of the medieval stonemasons who built the cathedrals and castles. There are about two hundred thousand Freemasons in the UK. The Freemasons have four important values that help define their path through life: integrity, friendship, respect, and charity.

"I supplied drugs for a man who was high up in the Freemasons. He would get seventy kilos from me every Thursday like clockwork. Sometimes I would not get paid. I was told by my drug contacts not to worry about it, and I didn't. That's how powerful the Freemasons were.

"I was introduced to the Freemason contact by my former colleague from the Office Care cleaning company, a French man named Mario Binasco. His office was located near the Liverpool Street Underground Station.

"I went to the meeting with a beautiful blonde Colombian woman. We arrived Friday evening about 8 p.m. at a pub close to Holborn Station. We went straight into the bar and ordered some beers. Soon a man came from behind the bar and introduced himself, telling us to follow him upstairs to a room. But it was more than a room. It was a very spacious and comfortable office. Two other men were there. They were very friendly and started to talk about business.

"The Colombian girl was not fully aware of my business, so I had to stop them. I asked one of them to go with her to the bar and have a drink. Once they left, we continued talking. We spoke about many things.

"They offered me an original British passport free of charge, but I declined. I never did get a British passport. They said it took twenty days to get one, but sometimes it took three months, and I could not be without my passport for that long. I don't think it would have made any difference if I had gotten one. But it would have given them more control over me. When you are a criminal, it is better to be a foreigner. If you want to deal in drugs in Colombia, it is better that you are American.

"When I went downstairs to the bar, the Colombian girl who came with me was hugging and kissing the other man. They had agreed to spend the night together, so I left the pub and drove home on my own.

"Weeks later, a parcel from Colombia, sent by my friends Pedro and Carlos, arrived at the port of Southampton in the English Channel. I wasn't familiar with how the security operated in that city. So I contacted my ex-associate Mario Binasco for information. He introduced me to a British police officer, who said he had some colleagues who would help me with security and information. I agreed to work with them, but I made it crystal clear that I would never meet them.

"Since one of my golden rules was to avoid disclosing any important information through any communication devices (mobile phones, computers, etc.), whenever I needed to receive or pass information, I always used women, especially escort girls or top-class prostitutes, to travel from one city to another or from one country to another. They carried a piece of paper tucked in their handbag. It had all the information they needed. They would keep it in their handbag, normally inside a pen or their lipstick.

"The girls would arrive at the city or country and go to a hotel. Hours later, they would call me or the person receiving the message and report in. Then the customer would arrive. He would pick up the piece of paper with the information and leave.

"This meant that the important information went straight to the person who needed it. Only two people in the world were aware of the information: the sender and the receiver. The chances of something going wrong were lessened. Later, when I was being followed by the British police, they would see me enter different hotels, restaurants, and pubs to meet these girls. They would check the girls' background and confirm that they were escorts and prostitutes. The police collected what they thought was evidence against me. They saw me in different places and with different girls from many places (Colombia, Brazil, Spain, Italy, and the UK). All they learned was Jesus was with a prostitute in a hotel. Jesus was with an escort at a bar. Jesus was with a prostitute at a restaurant, and so forth. It was not something the authorities could use in court against me.

"A few days later, I received a call from a Spanish girl asking me to meet her at the bar in the Hilton Hotel in Trafalgar Square in Central London at 6 p.m. As I normally did, I arrived at the hotel bar an hour early to look around and become familiar with the place and the surroundings. Something that was very important in my organization was that after we set up the time, day, and place for a meeting, we would not use any communication device.

"I went to the bar, ordered a beer, and took a seat. We did our best to make sure no one was aware of the meeting. Just before 6 p.m., I noticed a very elegant lady entering the bar. She had a Latina look to her. She looked at me. I smiled and said in Spanish: '*Estas muy bonita*' (you look beautiful). She smiled and answered in Spanish: '*Gracias.*' I offered her a drink. She ordered a glass of red wine, and we started talking and laughing about various things. After a few beers and some wine, we went upstairs to her room. I can't really describe what occurred between us. Let's just say it was all pleasure.

"Later, she said she had no idea where the document for me was. I started looking for it and found it inside her lipstick, a very small piece of paper with handwriting saying the date, time, container, number, and name of the ship, and the location and quantity of the cocaine inside the container. Only two people in the world were aware of this information, my friend in Colombia and me. It was totally safe.

"Three days later, I contacted the British police officer and asked him if it was possible for him to arrange a check of the port where the container had arrived. Without giving him information about the container or the parcel, I told him I wanted to go there to have a look around the area. I was casing the area for future work. He agreed to do it.

"At the same time, I sent Tito and Beto close to the area, as the container was already at the warehouse. I gave the green light to the person in the warehouse to go to the meeting point and hand over the parcel to Tito and Beto, who were waiting. There was a police car around, but it did not seem to pose a problem to us.

"Everyone proceeded as planned, and I received two cotton bags, each containing twenty blocks of cocaine, forty in total. Another door had been opened for future drug smuggling.

"Several weeks later, another parcel arrived, exactly the same as before, and because I had built trust with the police officer, I asked him to meet Tito in a supermarket close to Swiss Cottage Station. At the same time as their meeting, I was with Elsy in a coffee shop opposite the supermarket watching everything, Tito was already in the supermarket when two police officers arrived, parking their car, and went into the supermarket. I could not see what happened inside, but twenty minutes later, I saw the two officers walk out with grocery bags from the market. Five minutes later, Tito emerged and headed toward the underground station to go home. Their meeting was a success.

"The next day, a Brazilian woman called me to arrange a meeting. We met at the bar at her hotel in Central London. I took her to a restaurant close by. Later, we went back to the hotel where we had a few drinks and enjoyed a nice, short time together. She then handed me a pen and said it was a present for me. I went to the bathroom and broke the pen open. Inside was a handwritten piece of paper with the information about the new container, giving the name of the ship, arriving time, container number, location and quantity of cocaine inside the container, and the mobile number of the person inside the warehouse who would collect the parcel. Everything I needed was there.

"On the day of the collection, I sent Tito to pick up the parcel from the person at the warehouse and then drove back to London. However, just before entering into the metropolitan area, Tito contacted the police officer, who was on my payroll, and gave him the parcel that he had to take to the supermarket, which was close to our stash house in Hampstead, West London. Beto met the police officer inside the supermarket, and they swapped bags. Then Beto went back to the stash house. We did this for several months.

"I eventually had three police working for me. They would pick up the parcels and take them to a supermarket and make the transfer. I never met them. I never wanted to meet them in person. I would only talk with them by phone. They actually came to me through recommendation. Later, they were arrested about a week after my arrest.

"One of them made a terrible mistake. He was taking the cocaine and giving it to his son, who sold it in a bar. The police were aware that cocaine trafficking was going on in that bar. They put the son of the policeman under surveillance and a wire on the police officer's vehicle. Everything he said was recorded. They learned that he was getting the cocaine from his father. It was really stupid. The corrupt cop should have been aware that the police were watching the bar.

"The prosecution tried to use the recorded conversations as evidence in my case. The corrupt police officers (three in total) were arrested, but they had no idea who I was because I would never meet them. At no time were they linked to me. The police officers were charged and sentenced to eight years in prison. Later, however, the recorded conversations were dropped from my case because of a lack of evidence.

"Interestingly, most of the evidence about their police involvement with my organization eventually disappeared. Nigel Dean from Edward Fail and Waterson Solicitors, Southeast London, was my solicitor. He's now a magistrate judge. He is fully aware of my whole case, especially the corrupt British police involvement with the evidence.

"I also had a couple of police officers, a man and woman, working for me in Gatwick Airport. They were also arrested for a stupid mistake. My people would smuggle the cocaine and money in their luggage, and the corrupt police officers would wave them through. I did that for years. We were able to get at least a ton of cocaine into the UK that way.

"But the airport was too good of a thing to last. One of my men was hanging around the airport, and the police spotted him on the cameras. Anyone hanging around would be suspicious. They arrested him.

"The two corrupt police officers were also arrested and got fifteen years. They served about half their sentence. I'm sure the corruption is still going on, given the money involved. It's a big temptation for anyone, no matter who they are.

"In early 1997, I started to send a lot of money through a company called Condor Services. The money was sent by *giros* (money transfers) to Colombia to someone who worked for us. Fernando Caranza Reyes, who later became a police informant, was the man in charge of the *giros*. He would later be a witness against me. The man in charge of Condor Services was his uncle, Lobin Reyes. Fernando had to be careful about the amount of money he sent via the *giros* in case his uncle found out.

"A few years later, I had a meeting with Fernando in a bar around the Holborn area in London. Fernando told me that he had everything ready to start doing the *giros* in big amounts, but he needed to create a company in London. I agreed to set up a company for him to launder money.

"Fernando explained to me that he had family members in Cali and Pereira, Colombia, who were ready to work with us. His uncles, father-in-law, and the other in-laws— indeed, practically all members of his family—were given training in how to contact hundreds of people who were of modest means. They would give the *giros* their names and ID numbers. On the UK end, we invented a fictitious name and an ID number for the sender.

"We split the money into five-hundred-pound deliveries, the maximum that could be legally sent under Colombian law. The details of the sender and receiver were sent to Fernando's family in Colombia, and they, in turn, would contact the person and take them to the *giros* office to pick up the money. They would then give the money to Fernando's family. The receiver would get a very small profit, but it was good money for them, and they were willing to do it over and over again.

"In early 1999, Pedro and Jose, my two friends in Colombia, informed me that I needed to get ready because, in the next three months, between four or five big parcels would arrive. They would contain cocaine imprinted on tons of plastic rolls. I would have to take the product out of the plastic. This would require a chemist, who my friends in Colombia sent from Colombia to the UK.

"The work was laborious and could take weeks. So I went with Tito and Elsy to Bayswater area where there was a shop that sold the chemicals. We went into the shop basement looking for what we needed. I found it on a stand. It was being sold in bottles. Elsy picked up a bottle and went to buy it while Tito and I left the shop. Elsy met us outside, and we drove away to a safe house where we checked the contents of the bottle.

"The results came out well. Now the challenge was to buy the quantity I needed; I would have to purchase hundreds of bottles. I decided to get Elsy's sister involved and put her in charge of buying the bottles. I got many different people to buy one or two bottles. I paid them twenty pounds for the bottle. They sold for about seven pounds. About two months later, the shop ran out of the chemical, but I had enough to start my work.

"I now needed somewhere to do the work, so I went looking in the countryside for a safe location. I found a very good house, located outside the Brentwood area. There was a way out from the back street and no neighbors were close by. I bought it for seventy thousand pounds and put it under Beto's Spanish name. I also bought a static holiday caravan, which was located in Clacton-on-Sea, about one-hour drive north of the house. I went there hundreds of times with friends and family.

"There was an important reason why I needed the caravan. It was on the same road as the house, and whenever I got suspicious about something, I would not drive to the house but go to the caravan. So, if I was seen in that area, I had a reason for being there. I was going to and from my holiday caravan.

"About two months later, a lorry with a container full of plastic and other goods arrived. It went through the motorway M25 and stopped close to a Shell petrol station at Junction 28. Tito, Elsy, and Beto arrived at the petrol station. Elsy went to the petrol station's coffee shop to look out for anything suspicious. Everything was fine, so they drove to the lorry and started to unload the big plastic rolls into the van they had rented. They ended up with about fifteen rolls, each weighing about thirty kilograms.

"They then drove to the town parking and left the van for a few hours. Later, another driver took the van and drove it to a street closer to the house where the job would be done. Late at night or early in the morning, the van was moved to the back entrance of the house and unloaded.

"A man named Enrique was the chemical expert. He arrived from Spain and went straight to work. He started in the early afternoon and finished about midnight. He filled up a tank with the chemical we had brought and warmed it up. He put the plastic inside for about four hours at a time. Then he took it out and washed it with another chemical. The water started to drain, leaving the wet cocaine that had sunk to the tank's bottom. Then he started to collect the cocaine from the bottom and put it into wooden modules. He then placed the cocaine into the microwave for a few seconds. He took the cocaine out and placed it under a strong light while constantly turning the cocaine until it became dry.

"The entire process took about fourteen hours. The final product ended up being blocks of cocaine. In all from one parcel, the chemist was able to get out ninety blocks, each weighing one kilogram each. After five days, the chemist was done and flew back to Spain. I then moved the cocaine to a stash house. We continued this job for several months with the same chemist. He was very careful. When he came to the UK, I always made sure we changed cars and mobile phones for every new shipment we handled.

"A few months later, a man named Carl, the one who started with a quarter kilo from Gospel Oak area, North London, rented a hotel to celebrate his birthday. He invited a lot of friends. During the party, he started to boast to his friends about how much money he had and that he had the one thing none of them had: the Colombian connection. This made a lot of people at the party really jealous of him. That same night someone snitched on him to the police. Early in the morning, he was at his flat sleeping when the police broke down his door and arrested him. They found five kilograms of cocaine in his flat's cooker.

"Carl owed me money. He told me that a very important person in the local drug business had my money and that he would only give the money to the main man, me. Carl gave me his number.

"A few hours later, I brought a brand-new mobile phone number and called the number that Carl gave me. A very strong voice answered the phone. I explained to him that I was the man to whom he owed the money and asked him how I could collect my £140,000. He told me that he would only give the money to me and no one else, so we arranged a meeting for the next day in the early evening. The next day, I went with Tito to a corner pub next to Mornington Crescent Underground Station around 6 p.m.

"When I entered the pub, I noticed a table with two young black boys looking at us. We went inside, and I saw a massive black man. My instinct told me that he was the man with my money. So I approached the table and introduced myself. He told me his name was Michael. He stood up and shook my hand. He ordered some beers for me and Tito, and we began talking about different subjects.

"I mentioned to him that Mr. Big could not come to the meeting. Tito and I were the right-hand men of the Big Man, and we could talk for him. Michael was not happy and started to talk a lot of shit about Mr. Big. He said he had the money outside but would not hand it over to us, only to Mr. Big. He started speaking about Mr. Big, saying that he couldn't keep his word. In this kind of business, reputation is the most important quality you need to have because people will believe what you say and do what they are told.

"As Michael was bad mouthing the boss, me, Tito was nudging me under the table and looking towards my direction, waiting to see what I would do. The moment Michael started to talk about reputation, I immediately stopped him, raising my arm.

"Hold on, hold on," I said. "Listen, amigo, the big man, the real Mr. Big you are talking about is me. I'm the man. I'm Jesus Ruiz Henao."

"Michael froze and looked straight into my eyes. This massive man jumped from his chair, saying: 'It's you. It's you!' I stood up and told him to take a seat because people around were looking at us. He did. We sat down and continued talking. He told me he was the main man, and it was not good for Carl to try to go into business without him. That's why they wanted him out. They ended up reporting him to the police.

"He guaranteed I would not lose my money and that he would give me my £140,000 he was holding. He would also recover the money for the five kilos the police seized from Carl. He would deal directly with me from now on. I shook his hand and then followed two young black boys to a car. They handed Tito a bag with all the money inside. The £140,000 was there.

"I kept doing business with him for several years. I started small, but as time went by, I increased the amount. He would take up to fifty to a hundred kilos of cocaine at a time, and was always good for the payment. I lost contact with him because he got involved with another supplier. In any case, I decided working with him had become too dangerous.

"By now, we had reached the millennium, the year 2000, and I could see nothing but great things continuing to happen for me. Everything was going well. The authorities didn't have a clue about what I was doing."

SIX

BACK IN COLOMBIA

By the end of 2000 and into the beginning of the 2001, Jesus Ruiz Henao was at the height of his power. He was laundering millions of dollars but realized he needed professional help to handle the money. So he contacted Carlos Coronado, an expert money launderer who was recommended to him. Jesus operated his money laundering operation from a Colombia café in Archway, North London, called *La Gran Colombia*. This café bar was run by Fernando Carranza Reyes, who later became a police informant. It was opened in 2001 and shut down by the police in 2003.

Ruiz Henao: *"La Gran Colombia* was one of two restaurants I owned. The second restaurant was Latinos Number, located close to Liverpool Street. I opened it in 1998 to launder money through *giros,* or money transfers. Both restaurants were Colombian delicatessens that appealed to Latinos. We would fabricate names, putting five hundred pounds into another fictitious name in Colombia that was fabricated by us as well. We forged driver's licenses with the name. They would present the driver's license with that name and get the money.

"Everybody knew what was going on. We had more than a million deposit slips. It was stupid to keep that much paper, but I broke my own rule. Don't keep paper. I had a worker who decided to keep the slips. He didn't tell me, but when I was busted, the police found the slips. It was damning evidence. You try to tell your workers not to do things, but it is hard to make sure they don't do it. He made a mistake, but the truth is the business was getting more problematic the bigger I got. It was becoming much more difficult to watch everything. You can have ninety-nine good workers, but all it takes is one person to screw things up.

"Coronado was one of my three main money launderers. The other two were Tito and Jose. They were all very good."

Laundering money was a constant challenge. Millions of pounds were flooding in. So Jesus bought a betting company in 1999 called Eurochance, which operated in London, Madrid, and Paris, and served to launder money. Jesus also owned a consumer goods company in Spain called *Compartiendo*. Both companies allowed Jesus to move his money around and keep one step ahead of the law.

Ruiz Henao: "I laundered my money through a variety of countries, including Panama, Switzerland, and the Cayman Islands. I used lorries to launder my money through Switzerland. The existence of the European Union helped me a lot. There was no border control. I would give a million or two pounds to a lorry driver, and he would take the money to Switzerland, where somebody would pick it up and go to the bank. The money would then disappear into numerous bank accounts.

"You hear how hard it is to move money from the drug trade. But I found it to be easy. The controls were much tougher before the 9/11 terrorist attack. You couldn't meet people or hang around a corner without worrying about cameras picking you up.

"I also stashed money in safe houses. I would rent an apartment, usually on the ground floor. It had to have security. I would bring boxes of money containing as much as five to ten million pounds.

"I had five guys delivering the cocaine. I would give them a thousand pounds for each kilo of cocaine they delivered. I would make about three thousand to five thousand pounds per kilo. I would make one hundred to two hundred deliveries a week. I didn't have to pay taxes so I didn't have to keep any records. It is very dangerous to keep records or any piece of paper about an illegal business. I tried to keep the information all in my head.

"As for personnel, my men would never betray me. They had my trust. I was very loyal and sincere with them, and I was good at reading people. I could shake their hand, and I would know what kind of person they were. I studied people. I read hundreds of psychology books that helped me a lot. I wanted to know what made a man tick. But I still made a mistake once. I had a young boy working for me who gave up the safe house that had two million pounds stored in it. The boy was recommended to me, and unfortunately, I trusted the person who recommended him.

"With *La Gran Colombia* opened, it became easier to move the money. I got a new worker to handle the money, and he would collect and drop it off to Carranza Reyes at *La Gran Colombia*. We started to do between three hundred thousand to five hundred thousand pounds per week. In Colombia, Fernando's family collected the money from the receiver, and he would give it to my brother, Jairo, who, in turn, handed it to the patron. Sometimes I would use the money to help finance the next shipment.

"Carlos Coronado started meeting with people to pick up the money. He eventually met a Colombian man, who was gay, and recommended to us by a man from Cali. Because he had long hair we called him *La Peluda* (hairy). Coronado was right to be suspicious of the man. *La Peluda* brought the heat with him. The police were following him, and now they were following Coronado. We know the police took several photos of him moving bags of money into *La Gran*

Colombia. Coronado noticed he was being followed and flew to Cali, Colombia.

"I thought it best to stop sending money through *La Gran Colombia* for a few months. Fernando, however, was already heavily involved with a lot of people in sending money for them to Colombia. On 4 September 2003, I went to see Fernando at *La Gran Colombia* to ask about sending three hundred thousand pounds to Colombia. Fernando agreed to do it.

"A few days later, I went to Paris, and while there, I got news that Fernando was arrested in Colombia. Extradited to the UK in 2009, he pled guilty to money laundering and was sentenced to five and half years in prison. The police also seized *La Gran Colombia.* I was okay with this because I hadn't done anything with Fernando in a long time. I was sure that the police would find no evidence of my involvement with him. However, Fernando became a witness against me. In fact, his testimony was the most important evidence that the police had against me."

In early April 2001, while Jesus' new home in Hendon in Northwest London was being refurbished, he decided to travel to Colombia with his wife, daughter, and two-year-old son. Jesus put his brother-in-law, Mario Tascon, in charge of his organization while he was out of the country.

Ruiz Henao: "I know the press made Mario out to be a partner, but he didn't play a major decision-making role in my organization. My English was not very good. Mario spoke excellent English. He worked in a coffee shop, and I asked him to help me out. He became more and more involved in my organization. Sometimes I would travel, and I didn't want to go by myself, so I would ask him to come along to keep my company. Or else I needed someone to pick up some cocaine, and I would send him."

Mario would have to get Jesus' permission to make any changes while he was gone.

"I needed to stay in Colombia for two or three months because my partners Pedro and Jose and I were ready to send our first one ton of cocaine into the UK in one shipment. It wasn't an easy decision to go to Colombia. I was aware of the danger I would face from the *sicarios* who had wanted to kill me in 1995. They had forced me to flee the country. But business compelled me to go.

"I now had the money to buy a house in Pereira for us to stay in. I also bought a bulletproof 4x4 Toyota. We arrived in Bogota at around 11 p.m. One of my boys was waiting for us in a bulletproof Toyota and drove us straight to a hotel where we spent the night. I got an intelligence briefing on my security and felt satisfied that we were being taken care of well. I was very happy to see how Colombia had changed for the better since 1995."

On 7 August 1998, Andrés Pastrana, a member of the Conservative Party, was sworn in as the president of Colombia. Pastrana sought to bring about a peaceful resolution of Colombia's long-standing civil conflict and to cooperate fully with the United States in combating the trafficking of illegal drugs. Pablo Escobar and the Cali Cartel were both taken down by 1995, but the country's drug trade had continued unabated. The *Norte del Valle* Cartel and other drug trafficking organizations were quick to take advantage of the situation. As the Medellín and Cali Cartels fell, the guerrillas and paramilitaries filled the void, causing the international street prices of cocaine to drop and the supply to pace with an ever-rising demand.

In 1998, Orlando Henao Montoya, *El Hombre del Overol* (the Overalls Man), leader of *Norte del Valle* Cartel (NDVC), was murdered in prison in retaliation for a hit on Cali Cartel chief Helmer Pacho Herrera, whom Henao Montoya believed was cooperating with the DEA. Wilber Varela, alias *Jábon,*—another ex-policeman, who had been in charge of the organization's assassins—took control of the NDVC with the support of Lorena Henao Montoya, the sister of Henao Montoya and then wife of imprisoned NDVC leader Ivan Urdinola, alias *El Enano* (the Dwarf). However, the organization began to break up as *Jábon* and his allies were challenged by a faction led by Diego Montoya Sanchez, alias Don Diego.

In 2002, the NDVC was concerned about Colombia reintroducing extradition for drug traffickers, and this lead to a permanent breakup of the cartel. The US indicted several NDVC leaders. Others were so concerned by the turn of events that they began to turn themselves in voluntarily. Tensions were high, and they reached a breaking point when one of Don Diego's main allies, Victor Patiño Fomeque, *El Quimico* (the Chemical), met with DEA agents to negotiate his surrender. However, he was arrested instead and extradited to the US where he began to cooperate with the DEA.

After a failed hit on Varela left him in the hospital with multiple gunshot wounds, he declared war on Diego Montoya, whom he held responsible for the attack. Meanwhile, another Don Diego ally, Miguel Solano, began informing on his associates to the DEA. When *Jábon* found out, he had Solano killed. Don Diego, who had also been considering turning himself in, was apparently unaware Solano had been snitching and retaliated, launching a full-scale war between the factions. The bloody war pitted the military wings of their operations—*Jábon*'s *Rastrojos* and Don Diego's *Machos*—against each other. The conflict claimed an estimated one thousand lives between 2003 and 2004 alone.

The mafia war got more complicated when it got entangled with Colombia's Civil War. Don Diego reportedly allied himself with the leftist guerrillas of the Revolutionary Armed Forces of Colombia (FARC), while *Jábon* turned to the guerrillas' enemies in the right-wing paramilitary umbrella group, the United Self-Defense Forces of Colombia (AUC).

Ruiz Henao: "At the time of my return to Colombia in 2001, the drug lords didn't go round as they would in the past with four or more trucks full of bodyguards to show off their power. No longer did they kill for the hell of it. People still got killed but for a reason or because they crossed the line in a deal. Now I noticed the Colombians running the cocaine business were more professional and all the people involved looked like businessmen. They didn't need to go around killing or showing off their power. They became more serious in the business and a lot more careful. I also noticed that the cocaine production was now in the hands of the guerillas and the paramilitaries, and they were the ones holding all the power in the production of this business. It was a monopoly."

The drug trade had exploded between 1990 and 2001, and it permeated all layers of society, including the guerrillas and violent right-wing paramilitaries. The major guerrilla group FARC initially distanced themselves from drug trafficking, but in the 1980s, they adopted a tax called "grammage" that taxed activities related to illicit trade in the territories under FARC control, such as crops, processing laboratories, and the exportation of drugs. Drug trafficking cartels did not welcome this initial guerrilla foray into the drug trade, and they soon joined forces with the paramilitaries to fight the guerrillas.

FARC's growing role in Colombia's drug trade put it in conflict with the drug trafficker-paramilitary alliance and led to a resurgence of violence in Colombia. With the takedown of the Medellín and Cali Cartels, an opening was created for paramilitary groups, which controlled northern Colombia (the key transnational smuggling route), to take over the international cocaine trade. In 2001, Colombian government sources estimated that at least forty percent of all cocaine exports from Colombia were controlled by far-right paramilitary groups. In stark contrast, only 2.5 percent were controlled by FARC.

Ruiz Henao: "To my surprise, I was told that Mico, the head of the *sicarios*, was arrested in Pereira for murder and sent to *La Picota*, a high-security prison in Bogotá. After two years in prison, he began to fight someone from the guerillas. He was stabbed to death in the prison. This was sad news, but it was good for me since I was no longer under any death threat. The *sicarios* were still around but easier to deal with since Mico, the boss, wasn't around anymore.

"The day after my arrival in Colombia, I travelled to Pereira with my family. We set ourselves up in the new home. I bought a small Ford Fiesta, which I used to travel around the city. Everything had changed for the better and was improving. I went to see my brother, Jairo, and everything was good with him. In the evening, I went out for some drinks and to get a better look at Pereira. Later that night, I enjoyed some dancing at a night club and then went home to rest and be ready to start business in the morning.

"At 10 a.m. the next morning, I took my family to visit my wife's sister, who lived in a very popular area of Pereira. We went inside and greeted the sister and her family. A few minutes later, the best and flashiest cars in all of Pereira started to arrive and parked outside on the street. My old boss Sergio arrived. I went to the door and opened it for him. We shook hands, and he gave me a big strong hug. Then he came in the house and sat down. He ordered one of his bodyguards to go and bring my favorite whiskey, Chivas Regal 21.

"We started talking about many things, laughing and enjoying each other's company. Then I received a phone call from my aunt who lived across the street. She asked me: 'Son, who are all the people in the expensive cars on our street, and are they all here to see you?' I just laughed and told her: 'Don't worry, auntie. They are all my friends.'

"A few hours later, Sergio invited me to one of his villas close to the city. I left my family with my wife's sister and went with Sergio. When we arrived at the villa, everything was prepared and ready for my arrival. There were plenty of beautiful young girls in miniskirts waitressing. In the Jacuzzi, there were three of the most beautiful girls I had ever seen waiting on me. They said that they were my servants. We drank whiskey and ate food. After a lot of partying and dancing, I felt tired and went to bed with so many girls that I wasn't able to count them. It was a night to remember. Early in the morning, my boss left to go to another city, and I was taken back to my house where my wife was waiting. She wasn't happy, but we worked things out.

"Later that day, I went to see Pedro and Jose, who were waiting for me. We needed to make the necessary arrangements so that we could get everything ready for our travel to the port of Barranquilla. We needed to get our ton of cocaine in route to mainland Europe and then into the UK.

"Two days later, we travelled by car from Pereira to Barranquilla in the north. It was about an eighteen-hour drive, which made for a two-day journey. Whenever we travelled by road in Colombia, there would always be police stops. If they saw two or three men in the car, they would get suspicious and start asking questions. But if we had girls in the car, it would seem natural to the cops, and they wouldn't stop us. For this reason, we hired two escort girls to travel with us. After the long journey, we arrived to Barranquilla and booked ourselves into a hotel.

"The next day, we moved closer to the port and had breakfast. We waited for the call that would allow us to enter the port. It was very difficult to get into the port, but about an hour later, one of the port managers called and invited us in. The port manager was well aware of my drug business, and he knew that the police and customs were present. We followed him to a massive container storage area where, after a few minutes of moving around, he called one of the port workers, who was also aware of our business. The manager told the worker to open the container in which we had the ton of cocaine stored. The worker complied and opened it up, but inside the container were only wooden pallets with boxes stacked on top of them.

"Then another worker brought a forklift and moved some of the pallets out the way. We went inside and saw that part of the container floor was removed. It had fake flooring, and when we inspected it, we could see the cocaine with our trademark. We used car logos for our trademark, and on this shipment, we used the Mercedes logo stamped on each of the kilos. Everything was put back into place, and the container number was given to us.

"We went back to our hotel. Each one of us—Pedro, Jose and I—all had the numbers and necessary documents. Everything was in place for our first ton of cocaine to be delivered to the UK. We were excited. That night we forgot about the business and celebrated. The next day we returned to Pereira. A day later, we met again to look into the numbers and the cost of shipment."

Here are the figures Jesus tabulated for the drug shipment expenses:

- Production of one thousand kilos of cocaine: £500,000
- Payment of land transport: £100,000
- Payment of port officials: £200,000
- Payment to port workers: £100,000
- Payment to ship company: £500,000
- Payment to ship workers: £100,000

Ruiz Henao: "We had already spent £1.5 million, and we still needed to pay for unloading the cocaine and transporting it into the UK. Pedro, Jose, and I raised the money, but when the load arrived in the United Kingdom, the expenses were to be my responsibility. We expected the cargo to leave in the next two weeks. Meanwhile, I had to return to London so I could organize things on that side.

"A week later, I sent my family to the UK while I remained in Bogotá waiting for the ship to depart. I booked myself into the *La Fontana* Hotel, which was located north of Bogotá. Four days later, I was informed that the ship had departed from Spain and would stop in Amsterdam, Netherlands, where the container would be unloaded. It would take about three weeks to arrive in the UK.

"I booked my flight to Madrid. I arrived in Madrid the next day and booked myself into the *Husa Princesa* Hotel in Central Madrid. That night I went out to a club with one of my workers who was in Madrid. I met a fantastic Colombian girl named Gloria, who became part of my romantic life. We were out all night, and in the early morning, we went back to my hotel. She stayed with me the whole time I was there.

"Two days later, I travelled with her to Barcelona to meet the Spaniards, who were my contacts and were already aware about the cocaine cargo at the storage place in Amsterdam. I met them and gave them all the necessary information required to do their jobs. They would use one of the lorries from the company to pick up the load and transport it into the UK full of vegetables and fruits.

"After everything was organized, I went back with Gloria and we headed for Peníscola, a town located on the Costa del Azahar, north of the Serra d'Irta along the Mediterranean coast. It is a popular tourist destination. I booked us into the best hotel there. Two days later, we returned to Madrid, and I rented an apartment for Gloria in the center of Madrid. I also used the apartment as a stash house to store money. I bought Gloria a new mobile phone and gave the Spaniard her contact, telling him to contact only Gloria and not me.

"A week later, I returned to the UK, back to my family at our new home in Hendon. The next day, I got information from Gloria that the Spanish men were in Amsterdam, already waiting. I called my brother, William, and instructed him to travel to Amsterdam and book himself into the same hotel as the Spaniards. He would be my eyes and ears, watching and checking to be sure everything would go as planned.

"My brother, William, left that day, and later on in the day, Mario, my brother-in-law, set up a meeting with Tito, Beto, and a new worker called Wilmar. We met at a strip club near Liverpool Street called Browns. After a few drinks, I instructed them to give themselves plenty of time to be ready for the arrival of the ton of cocaine. I gave them enough money to buy two nearly brand-new cars and handed them brand-new mobile phones and a set of new pagers. They would use the technology only for the job. They were to be on call 24/7. They had the necessary information but only what they needed to know. Then we enjoyed the rest of the night and the early morning hours together before going home.

"The next day, I went with Mario and Elsy to buy two more cars. I needed four in total. Each one would be used to carry two hundred and fifty kilograms of cocaine. William, my brother, reported that everything went well and that the trucks had left Amsterdam and were on their way to the UK. The Spaniard contacted Elsy, who wanted to meet in a restaurant near Tottenham Court Road in Central London at lunch time. I went to the restaurant with Elsy. We ordered lunch and then received a message from the Spaniard, giving us his description so that we could spot him when he came into the restaurant.

"We looked around and saw him, by himself, having lunch on his own. Elsy got up and approached him. After a few words, Elsy invited him to our table. He asked for the car keys and plate numbers. We gave him what he wanted. He told us where to leave the cars. We were to do that before sunset. He told us that the cars would be parked in the same place after midnight. Everything had gone well, he assured us.

"Minutes later, he left. I contacted Tito and told him about the delivery of the cars. He was to keep the keys so that he could pick up the car later in the night. Tito, Beto, Wilmar, and Coronado drove the cars to the place, one by one, and Elsy and her sister stayed in a pub nearby keeping an eye on the cars. The cars were picked up by the Spaniards, and at about 1 a.m., the first loaded car arrived. Half an hour later, Tito arrived and got in the car. He drove it to the stash house in Tottenham, North London.

"The next loaded car arrived. Beto drove it to the stash house in West Hampstead. The third and fourth car arrived at the same time. Wilmar drove one to the stash house in Russell Square, and Coronado drove the last car to the area of Putney Bridge, a new safe house. All the cars were unloaded, and the cocaine was stored in the kitchen. I was informed that everything went as planned. I was really happy. I went back home to get some rest.

"It was the first time that amount of cocaine, a ton of it, was imported into the UK. The next day at midday, I sent Tito to *La Paloma* with ten kilograms. I followed up by sending Beto with another ten kilograms to a Scot contact and Wilmar with ten kilograms to a contact in Gospel Oak. Less than half an hour after the deliveries were done, I received messages from my contacts asking for more. They said that the quality was really good.

"*La Paloma* sent one million pounds in advance for more. I authorized that we give him three hundred kilograms. There were two more buys, and I sent them two hundred and fifty kilograms each. At about 5 p.m., all the cocaine was gone. It was so exciting. This was my biggest and fastest cocaine sale I had done in a single day. But now we had to collect the money and send it back to Colombia.

"For the next few days, my people—Tito, Beto, Wilmar, Elsy, and Coronado—ran all around London, from one place to another, collecting and stashing the money. It was remarkable. We collected it all. Millions of pounds were stashed in our safe houses. There was so much money that the stash houses became full. I needed to do something about it."

At the end of March 2001, Jesus' friend Pedro in Colombia was under surveillance by American intelligence. Later, his son was arrested and sentenced to twenty years in prison for planning to import cocaine into the US. Pedro traveled to Puerto Rico, where he always stayed at the same hotel because a few of his friends liked to stay there. A hotel doorman became very friendly with Pedro and started to speak to him about the drug business, claiming that he had a lot of buyers in the UK and a good transportation system. He also told Pedro that he would be going to the UK for a modeling competition.

Ruiz Henao: "Pedro, without consulting me, gave the man the telephone number he used to contact me. Luckily when I contacted anyone abroad, I used one number only for that person. So if that number got intercepted, there was no link to anyone or anything else, other than one person. About three weeks later, I spoke with Pedro. He talked about the Puerto Rican man, whom he nicknamed The Model. He highly recommended him to me. He told me that he knew the Model for about five years and had already done some business with him. I believed what Pedro told me, so I agreed to meet the Model when he came to London.

"The Model phoned me the day he came to London. He told me he was really looking forward to seeing me and that he wanted to meet me as soon as possible. This would give him time to do some sightseeing. 'Would it be possible to meet that day at lunch time in a restaurant near London Bridge?' he asked me.

"I agreed to meet. The next day, I asked my in-law, Mario, to attend the meeting with me. Before we arrived, the Model called me to change the meeting place to a bar restaurant in the same area as our original meeting site. When we entered at the new meeting site, the bar felt weird. It had very few customers and only about three tables. There were two people present: the Model, who sat with another man.

"When they saw us enter, the Model gave us a friendly wave. As I walked toward them, I sensed that someone else was watching us. I arrived at the table and shook their hands. They offered us a drink. We took a seat and ordered beer.

"We started talking about different things, trying to break the tension in the atmosphere. The Model did the talking, while his friend sat quiet. The friend kept looking around and behind us. I looked at him and had a sudden bad feeling that he was a cop. We started to talk about the drug business. I portrayed myself as just a worker who didn't have the authority to make any final decisions. I explained that the main boss of our organization was in Spain and that he would be the only one who could approve any deal we worked out. He kept saying they had a great transportation system that could deliver any quantity. But then the man with the Model began to speak up. He asked silly questions like 'How is the cocaine packed?' and 'How will I deliver it to their company?'

"I had heard enough. I trusted my instincts. I looked at Mario, and, in a very quiet voice, said: 'Let's go.' The Model noticed my change in mood and changed the subject. Then he said: 'I was trying to contact you earlier, but I think you were out of the country.' I thought to myself: 'How does he know this?' and 'Why did he think this?'

"Mario and I stood up. We shook their hands. I said to them: 'Listen, this is not for me. I was here for my boss, but I don't think that he would be interested in talking with you. We have nothing more to speak about.' They just sat in silence and looked at each other. Mario and I left. This was one of the most stressful moments in my life. I was really scared.

"Years later, in 2003, when I was arrested and we saw the evidence in the case, it was confirmed that the Model, a Puerto Rican, was an informant with the American DEA.

He had managed to infiltrate Pedro's organization and was in London working with the British police. In early 2004, Pedro was arrested in Peru and sentenced to fifteen years for drug offenses. Pedro became very ill in prison, and four years later, he died while still inside."

SEVEN

IN HIGH GEAR

By the early 2000s, Jesus Ruiz Henao was running a smooth, efficient business, albeit illegal, which was making hundreds of millions of dollars. He was operating like a major corporation that a CEO would envy. At the height of his organization, he had from sixty to eighty people working for him in the UK and at least another twenty thousand people in Colombia, directly and indirectly, most of them involved with the *giros* (money transfers), laundering millions of pounds. According to British authorities, Jesus was bringing into the UK 1.5 tons of cocaine worth a cool £100 million on the street. Profits were hard to assess, but some estimates put them at £350 million in thirteen years. It was easy to make a deal since the cocaine was so plentiful. Many a time, all it would take would be a twenty-minute phone call.

Jesus used several different inventive methods for shipping his drugs. They included putting the drugs in mustard or jam or fruit to put sniffer dogs off the scent. As we have seen, he would also do the time-consuming task of ingraining the cocaine into clothing and plastic.

Ruiz Henao: "We liked to hide the drugs in fish that was iced down. We smuggled hundreds of kilos that way. I never had any problems. We also had some of our couriers swallow condoms containing money. It wasn't dangerous like swallowing bags of cocaine. We didn't use the swallowing method for cocaine, although we could have. The couriers were usually young. Many would take any kind of risk, including swallowing cocaine, to move the drug."

Much of the cocaine was shipped from Colombia to off the coast of Spain, where it was normally brought ashore in small boats. The Ruiz Henao organization repackaged the drugs, which were then sent to London, using cars, lorries, and couriers, and put in safe houses. The drugs were now ready for redistribution throughout the country. Every major city in the UK was targeted. The drugs were then sold to British crime groups.

Ruiz Henao: "When a shipment was being sent, I would get a message from a drug courier, usually a woman, often a prostitute from Spain. She came to London and booked herself into a hotel. She would then contact me and ask if I was going to take her out. I would say: 'Yeah, yeah, I will pick you up.'

"We went out, partied, came back to the hotel, shagged, and then she gave me the message. The note said the shipment was ready for delivery and gave the time and date when that would happen. The next message would come in about three or four months. Most of my shipments came by sea, but sometimes I used planes. We would fly drugs from Holland into the United Kingdom to a small airport at Luton.

"Smuggling drugs is tougher than it looks. It's not easy to move drugs from Colombia. It took so long to arrange a shipment. That is why big shipments were favored. The authorities would maybe catch a shipment or two. That was about it. Drug trafficking is a very good business."

At first Jesus worried about other gangsters moving in on him, but he recognized that as long as he kept a low profile, he would have little to worry about. With whomever he dealt, Jesus would tell them that he was just a messenger for Mr. Big.

Ruiz Henao: "I was always working. I would get information that a package was arriving in the United Kingdom at a certain time. I never knew until the last moment when or where that would be. I would have my cars ready. On one occasion, for example, it was seven o'clock in the evening, and a Spanish man showed up. I met him at a bar. He said I would need four cars. I put him in contact with one of my boys, who went with the Spaniard and got him four cars. The transfer of the cocaine was then made. For security reasons, we always had two sets of keys for the car. I went to bed. Around four o'clock in the morning, I was awakened. The cocaine had arrived. Each car carried about two hundred and fifty kilos each.

"Later, I went to the stash house to check on the delivery. I never used my own car, and I never went directly to a safe house. I used a lot of diversionary moves—for example, driving the car around and stopping for coffee—before I went to the stash house. Normally it would take me forty-five minutes to get there, but given all the diversion, it would take me three to four hours. I was very careful to make sure I was not followed. It's tough because it seems every corner in Britain has a camera. You can't get away from surveillance.

"I didn't really know how the cocaine was coming in or where it was going. In the drug business, the less you know, the longer you live. If you know too much, you could be in trouble. If something goes wrong, they want to know who knows.

"I kept the same approach for hiring anybody that worked for me. When I wanted to hire somebody, I really checked them out, just as I would if I had been running a legit company. I would find out where they liked to hang out. Then I would go there, buy something to drink, and check them out. I would see how they acted. I tried to get all the background information I could find on them: where they went to school, where they worked. I never introduced myself to them, never let them see my face. They never knew who I was.

"I hired many people from Colombia who were well recommended. They would fly to London, and after applying for and receiving refugee status, I would hire them. I never had any problem getting them into the country. The British immigration system was very lax in those days.

"I had to stay on top of my business. I worked from 8 a.m. to 10 p.m., seven days a week, mostly out of my house. I spent about half an hour each morning giving out instructions to my men. There was so much to the illegal cocaine trade. It was just like a regular business, except I was selling an illegal product. I had to meet people and arrange and negotiate deals, get the cars to move the product, then distribute it, figure out how to handle the money, and so forth. I never used the same cars. I would buy the cars from different places, a process that was very time consuming. I sold the cars after I used them once or twice. Here I was, a poor guy with no education and born in the jungle, who was operating a multi-million-dollar drug empire and becoming the first billion-dollar cocaine dealer in UK history.

"Like any businessman, I paid taxes and tried to carry on a normal life. I liked to carry about five thousand pounds on me. I would stash about thirty thousand pounds in the car for emergencies. When I ran out of money, I would just go to the car and get some more. I tried avoiding the use of credit cards. I didn't want to create a paper trail that could lead to me.

"We sold a top-quality product. We didn't cut the cocaine. Today, they cut the cocaine two or three times and sell it to anybody for about ten pounds a gram. Most anybody has ten pounds in their pocket. I would sell my cocaine for sixty pounds a gram. You had to have money to buy my cocaine. Few teenagers have that kind of money. I didn't care because I tried to keep our cocaine away from teenagers and the schools."

So what did he do with the money? After all, he had more money than he could spend in several life times.

Ruiz Henao: "I liked the good life. I liked the best restaurants and the best hotels. When I went to a restaurant, I never paid the bill. One of my boys paid it. In that way, there would no paper connection to me. My boy would get all the attention, especially from the women who might be with us. They didn't know I was the big boss.

"I would rent a hotel in one of my boy's names. I made it difficult for the police to track me. They called me Mr. Big. Maybe they should have called me the Invisible Man. I didn't want to be popular. I just didn't want anybody to know who I was.

"I remember once in 2000, when I was on holiday in Brazil. It was the evening, and we were with these beautiful prostitutes at a barbecue beside a pool. I liked one of the girls, but she was focused on my man, who was paying the bills and looked like the boss. My man was the one carrying the money. There were a bunch of girls around him; I was having a whiskey. Finally I said: 'Fuck it. I want that girl.' But my boy was acting like the boss. I said: 'Listen, who is the boss here? I am the main man.' So the girl came to me. It was one of the few times that I blew my cover.

"I tried to keep my family out of my business. I had a good relationship with my wife. She had her own company, a beauty salon. I helped set it up. She never asked me any questions, so I didn't have to give her false answers.

"I was sending two million pounds a week through *La Gran Colombia* via *giros* to different people in Colombia. The people were contacted by Fernando Carranza Reyes, who gave them a small payment for their collaboration. I also put up five hundred thousand pounds in a gym bag and handed it to a lorry driver who took the bag back to mainland Europe. There, it was picked up from a very good contact, a man from Paris. I also gave two girls a million pounds twice a week and the money would be transferred to my contacts in Colombia. I used a bureau of exchange near Paddington in Central London called Spring Exchange. It was later shut down by the police, and the owner was arrested and sentenced for money laundering offenses. I exchanged pounds into dollars and put about five hundred thousand dollars into travel bags, which different contacts took to Colombia. We never lost any money.

"It usually took us around three weeks to collect and count the money. To get the cocaine into Europe from Colombia, we spent over £3.5 million, not including the payment to our Spanish associates, who helped distribute the drugs. That cost us about two thousand per kilo. The payment for the transport from the Netherlands to the UK cost another £1.5 million. So all together Jose, Pedro, and I spent about seven million pounds per shipment.

"If a shipment was worth twenty million pounds, you subtract the seven million pounds in expenses, and that would mean thirteen million pounds in profit split between the three of us. Each of us made about £4.3 million in profit; however, since I was the one responsible for everything in the UK (selling, collecting the money, and paying the workers), I was allowed to sell each kilo for twenty-three thousand pounds, which meant I made an extra three million to cover my risk. I used the extra three million to pay for the new cars, and I gave each of the drivers two hundred thousand pounds. In total, the expenses cost me about one million pounds, leaving me with an extra two million pound profit. Not bad for a day's work.

"As I always did after the hard and stressful work of dealing with a shipment, I gave my workers a few months off. I went traveling with some of my closest associates. On one occasion, I went to Rio de Janeiro, Brazil, for two weeks with close workers. In Brazil, I had a friend who I had done business with me. He lent me his luxury yacht and introduced me to a group of beautiful Brazilian girls. One of them was a singer who sung all of Shakira's songs.

There was another girl named Tersinha, a beautiful blonde Brazilian girl who became close to me and later on one of my lovers. She traveled with me many times to Europe. We went to Brazil in a yacht, dancing, drinking, and enjoying our time. A few weeks later, after all the partying, I returned to Madrid and stayed with Gloria for another few days before returning to London.

"For security reasons, I always traveled outside the UK to do my partying, so I would not attract a lot of attention from the authorities. Most of the time, I went to Spain. I tried to keep a low profile. As I said, I was the one who never paid, even though it meant I had a harder time getting the girls. This is something that always makes me laugh because it happens all over the world. I've been to over a hundred countries and in all of them, the majority of women were always attracted to the money. And I did spend the money. Some of my trips cost me more than a hundred thousand pounds.

"Gloria was the lady who became my girlfriend in Spain. I normally called Gloria to be my company, and she was there for me ready to travel to wherever I needed her. She accompanied me to many places on my travels. I stayed in her apartment whenever I went to Madrid.

"Many times she traveled several days before me, carrying the money we needed for our expenses, and to get things ready for a good time. I went several times to Paris, Madrid, Barcelona, Prague, and Rio de Janeiro to party and for holidays, and many other major cities for a short holiday, but I never partied in the UK, because I knew if I started partying or spending a large quantity of money, the authorities would check me out and become aware of my activities. This was later confirmed to me, unfortunately, once I got arrested.

"Sometime later, I received a parcel from Sergio, my boss in Colombia, containing three hundred kilos. He would ship a lot of drugs to me, sometimes hundreds of kilos.

One time, he lost more than two tons of cocaine and on another occasion a ton. He got into debt, and in 2012, he was murdered in Pereira.

"I sold the drugs and sent the money back to Colombia. At this point, I had all the contacts and the market to sell any quantity of cocaine. I had control over the market, and I was aware of where in the UK the demand was the highest. I split the three hundred kilos and sent it to where it was needed most: that is, to Liverpool, London, and Manchester."

The money was always a big challenge to move and deal with due to its big bulk and the quantity that had to be moved around. But something that changed the world happened in New York: the September 11, 2001, attacks, often referred to as 9/11. There were a series of four coordinated terrorist attacks by the Islamist terrorist group al-Qaeda against the United States on the morning of Tuesday, September 11, 2001. Al-Qaeda, (Arabic, *al-Qā'idah* [the Base]) is a broad-based militant Islamist organization founded by Osama bin Laden in the late 1980s.

The attacks resulted in 2,977 fatalities, over twenty-five thousand injuries, and substantial long-term health consequences, in addition to at least ten billion dollars in infrastructure and property damage. It is the single deadliest terrorist attack in human history and the single deadliest incident for firefighters and law enforcement officers in the history of the United States, with 343 and 72 killed, respectively. The United States government responded to the September 11 attacks by launching the War on Terror, which sought to undermine al-Qaeda and its allies. The United Kingdom became a US ally in its War on Terror.

Ruiz Henao: "The 9/11 terrorist event changed everything in our business, because police everywhere in the world became more alert and started investigating at a new level. People began to get stopped and searched in the UK, and some losses started to occur."

But according to Pete Walsh, War on Drugs expert and author of *Drug War: The Secret History*, 9/11 did not appear to have had any direct effect on the cocaine trade. While there was enhanced security and checks on commercial aviation, the bulk of the cocaine trade to Europe was by then via sea-bound.

Walsh: "The response to 9/11 had a more visible impact on the heroin trade: the subsequent invasion of Afghanistan by US and Allied forces led to some concerted, British-led efforts to tackle poppy/opium production there. These efforts ultimately failed.

"However, there is a case to be made that 9/11 indirectly weakened the United Kingdom law enforcement response to the cocaine trade. The scenario runs like this. In the mid-1990s, the British overseas spying agency, the Secret Intelligence Service, more commonly known as MI6 (think James Bond), found its traditional workload declining, with the fall of the Berlin Wall, the collapse of the Soviet Union, and the end of the Cold War.

"Casting around to remain relevant, it fixed on organized crime, and persuaded the government to give it a role assisting HM Customs and the police in that sphere, using its considerable capabilities and knowledge overseas. This was authorized by the Intelligence Services Act of 1994. It was particularly relevant to Colombia, where MI6 had a substantial presence in the British embassy in Bogotá, and where they worked closely alongside their law enforcement colleagues.

"After 9/11, however, MI6 suddenly had a new imperative: Islamic terrorism. While it continued to work in counter-narcotics, it was, understandably, no longer so big a priority. This may well have impacted on the United Kingdom's overall effort against the trade – but it is hard to say how much."

Ruiz Henao: "Two girls from Paris came to London and booked themselves into a hotel. The next day, they met with Tito, and he handed them £650,000 in a suitcase. They picked up the bag and returned to the hotel. The hotel staff reported them to the police because they saw them return with a heavy bag and got suspicious. The police arrived at their room and searched the bag. They found the money. The girls were arrested and the money seized. This was my first ever loss, costing me £650,000. However, the arrest and the money seized were never linked to me, not even to the evidence when I was arrested.

"From now on, it became very dangerous to go around the United Kingdom carrying a big bag of money or drugs due to how strict the police became because of the terrorist attacks. Soon after, another delivery boy, named, Edward Ocampo, was stopped by the police in Putney Bridge in Southeast London. They found thirty thousand pounds on him. He immediately panicked and gave the police all the information about the stash house from where he picked up the money. The British police ran to the stash house in Putney Bridge, Southeast London, and seized two million pounds and nine hundred thousand dollars. The two boys, Edward Ocampo and Uriel Ortiz, were arrested. It was another major loss.

"This time the police looked at the evidence for these two and found CCTV footage. The authorities saw the two meeting with me in a supermarket car park in North London a month before. This was not enough evidence to connect me to them because, at this time, the police weren't aware of me. In fact, this was the first time they had seen me.

"Uriel Ortiz was living in a council flat on the third floor. Two doors away, he had rented the flat where he stored the drugs. When he was arrested, there were fifty kilos of cocaine, but luckily, the police that searched his house didn't know about the stash house. Two days later, I sent my brother, William, wearing an electrician uniform, to the house, and he managed to enter through the window. He put the fifty kilos inside three bags and into the car. Then he drove away and left the car in a car park overnight.

"We had successfully recovered the fifty kilos and the seized money (two million pounds and nine hundred thousand dollars). It would have been my biggest money loss to date. At the time, the police bugged my car and heard me talking about the loss. Business started to become a little more dangerous, and I started to think about a retirement. First, however, I needed to sort a few things out."

EIGHT

THE INVESTIGATION

By the late 1990s, Colombian cocaine was flowing into the United Kingdom. Colombia had overtaken Peru as the world's biggest producer of the coca plant, controlling three-quarters of the totally cultivated area of coca production. The Medellín and Cali Cartels had been taken down, but the *Norte del Valle* Cartel and other smaller cartels, as many as twenty of them, had filled the vacuum. The fragmentation of the drug trade made it more difficult for the authorities to investigate.

By the early 2000s, however, British law enforcement was as good as it had ever been at combating the drug trade. One of the major reasons was that the cooperation between British law enforcement agencies had improved significantly.

Walsh: "The police and HM Customs were working better and more closely together than ever before, after a long and awkward period of intense rivalry. The British security and intelligence services – MI5, MI6, and GCHQ – were supporting them strongly, as were elements of the British Army, Royal Navy, and Royal Air Force, and the military special forces.

"Royal Navy warships regularly patrolled the waters of the Caribbean to intercept drug boats, often in collaboration with their partners in the DEA, while military spy planes and satellites were used to monitor ship movements from the air. The UK had developed a comprehensive network of drug liaison officers abroad, fighting the coke trade out of their embassies and consulates in numerous countries, from Argentina and Bolivia to Peru and Spain. These officers shared intelligence with local law enforcement, passing it to and from the UK for action, and sometimes funded training and covert activities in poorer countries, including telephone tapping and data mining.

"Britain was also a prime mover in MAOC, the Maritime Analysis and Operations Centre, a European initiative to counter the threat of South American cocaine crossing the Atlantic. Created in 2006 and based in Lisbon, Portugal, MAOC could call on a host of assets from various countries to trace, track and interdict vessels carrying cocaine, and was responsible for multi-ton seizures on a regular basis. Its executive director, Tim Manhire, was British.

"The results of all of this were a sustained number of seizures of huge amounts of cocaine, often several tons, every year throughout the early and mid-2000s. Most of these seizures were not made in the UK itself but en route, often on ships sailing to the coast of Spain, the most popular unloading spot for cocaine, and latterly, West Africa. This was in keeping with the UK policy of 'upstream disruption,' which was designed to disrupt the cocaine trade before the drugs could reach their ultimate destination."

Given Jesus Ruiz Henao's success in the drug trade, he had become more high profile than he suspected and was now on the radar of UK law enforcement. An investigation of had been ongoing, but the British authorities began to investigate him seriously when HM Revenue and Customs handed the Ruiz Henao case to the National Crime Squad of England and Wales (NCS) in late 2001.

Customs had decided to release the Ruiz Henao case to the NCS because it conceded that had it neither the resources nor the capability to handle a major drug trafficker like him. In the words of one British law enforcement officer, Ruiz Henao "was too smart for them."

The NCS was a British police organization which dealt with national and transnational organized and major crimes. It was formed in April 1998 after the amalgamation of six former regional crime squads. The NCS primarily dealt with organized crime, major drug trafficking, contract killing, arms trafficking, human trafficking, computer and high-tech crimes, money counterfeiting and laundering, extortion, kidnapping, and murder related to any of the above. It also augmented and supported regional forces throughout the UK. The NSC merged with parts of the HMCE and the National Criminal Intelligence Services on 1 April 2006 to become the Serious Organized Crime Agency.

Jesus Ruiz Henao is not impressed with the several and often confusing name changes of British law enforcement. He believes it is a ploy to cover up bureaucratic ineptitude.

Ruiz Henao: "They kept changing the names, it seemed, like every three or four years. The British law enforcement would make several mistakes, so they would change the name to cover them up. When they went to court, and they had to explain a screw up, the current agency would blame the previous agency. But they were really the same agency. I don't know whom they think they were fooling."

Stephen Lear, who, at the time of Jesus Ruiz Henao investigation, was employed on secondment to the NCS of England and Wales from the Metropolitan Police (also known as the London Police or Scotland Yard), sees nothing out the ordinary with the name changes.

Stephen Lear: "There were no doubt mistakes made as there always are in every walk of life. You have to add to that the politics in all this. The Serious Organized Crime Agency was a labor 'baby' under Tony Blair, designed to bring together all the different investigative agencies into one place: the NCS (Police), Investigations Division from

Her Majesty's Customs and Excise, National Criminal Intelligence Service and Immigration Enforcement Investigations. When they lost power, the Conservatives wanted the name changed to National Crime Agency, and they slightly changed the Agency's focus and priorities. I am sure you have seen similar name changes in US. It doesn't mean we are trying to cover up mistakes."

Nevertheless, the NSC was deadly serious about taking down Ruiz Henao. The case against him was code named Operation Habitat, and it came under the direction of Stephen Lear, Lear had joined law enforcement late, at twenty-eight years of age, but he rose rapidly through the ranks. Lear had six detectives working under him. He spent five years with the NCS, and the Ruiz Henao case was his first big one.

Lear: "Customs didn't have too much information about Ruiz Henao, so we pretty well had to start from scratch. We suspected him of drug trafficking, but nothing much else. We started off by trying to understand with whom he worked."

In February 2002, the British authorities went operational; that is, they moved from the intelligence gathering phase to operational phase where they actively began to surveil and wiretap Ruiz Henao.

On 16 May 2002, police stopped two of Ruiz Henao's associates, Pablo Emilio Aramburo and Walter Herrera, while driving a BMW on the City Road in Islington. While Aramburo, the driver, was speaking to one of the officers, Herrera was seen to reach from the front passenger seat toward a large green hold-all on the vehicle's backseat. The police seized the hold-all, opened it, and found a large package wrapped in plastic bags. Inside the bags were some large blocks of cocaine. Both Aramburo and Herrera were arrested for possession of a controlled substance with intent to supply.

Lear: "We arrested Pablo Emilio Aramburo, but we never induced into evidence the man's arrest. He was prosecuted purely on the basis of possessing five kilos of cocaine. We were able to tie Aramburo to Ruiz Henao, but that was about it. In the British legal system, there is a fine distinction between evidence and intelligence. You can't use intelligence in a court case."

Convicted on 10 February 2003, Walter Herrera got seven years because he decided to go to trial. The investigators continued to move in on the men around Ruiz Henao. In January 2003, they arrested Carlos Olner Castano Aguirre. When the investigators raided his house, they found two hundred thousand pounds, forged passports, and cocaine. The police established a direct link with five kilograms of cocaine, recovered from the vehicle occupied by Pablo Aramburo and Walter Herrera. Documentation was found implicating Castano Aguirre in the transfer of money to individuals in Colombia. He was accused of conspiring with Aramburo, Herrera, and with a person unknown, and sentenced to thirteen years in prison.

By this time, the investigators knew Luis Fernando Carranza Reyes was running the money laundering side of Ruiz Henao's drug business and having meetings with him. They had established a link between the money and the drugs. In March 2003, a year after their investigation began, the investigators began to employ listening devices in their investigation. In April 2003, William Ruiz Henao, Jesus's brother, was arrested at the Spanish lorry with seventeen kilos of cocaine and ninety thousand euros. The Ruiz Henao organization was cracking, but the time consuming, labor-intensive work was costly.

Lear: "The investigation of Ruiz Henao took considerable resources. We had three full teams of officers working on the case. One team would have four sergeants and twenty-four detectives. So there were at least seventy-five officers working on the case, and often it was not the only case we were working on. By the time of Ruiz Henao's arrest, between two hundred and two hundred and fifty officers were involved.

"We took about three months preparing for the case. We used the time consuming and manpower draining task of surveillance; that is, following Ruiz Henao and his associates around. We found out where the individuals lived, where they hung out, and what cars they drove. Our suspicion, gathered from evidence, was that Ruiz Henao was the head of organization. He was very smart in how he conducted himself. He and his associates looked like regular Joes. They showed no outward display of wealth. But when we checked Ruiz Henao's credit card records, we saw that his wife was spending a lot of money, and we determined that Ruiz Henao had no visible means of support. He was spending beyond his means, but where was the money coming from?

"We logged many miles in the investigation. We had to go to foreign countries like Spain and Holland, where there were drug seizures to see what evidence we could find to use against Ruiz Henao. That proved useful.

"We managed to get lawful permission to put a listening device in the cars driven by Ruiz Henao and Mario Tascon, his brother-in-law, who seemed to be Ruiz Henao's main man. They spoke Spanish and in code. We had to get a person to translate the tapes. We had the six detectives under me working on various parts of the investigation. When we needed to do surveillance, we would all get together. Of course, we were working on other cases as well, but gradually we were building intelligence on the Ruiz Henao organization.

"We faced some stiff challenges. Big criminals like him are very careful, so it's difficult to build evidence, prove that he was giving the orders, and show he was meeting with his men. Once we put a listening device in his car, we spent a lot of time following him around. They always spoke in code whenever they were doing something illegal. It took us a while to understand that. The challenge was to listen to what was being said and to tie that to criminal events happening within the group. For instance, when drugs were being seized, we had to listen for what was the reaction in the car we bugged. We had to verify who was speaking. To do that, we had to use voice recognition technology."

Eventually Operation Habitat came into contact with Operation Anuric, another major British law enforcement drug trafficking operation. Lear and his team learned that they also had the Ruiz Henao organization under investigation and were focusing on the money laundering part of his criminal activity.

A key member of Operation Anuric investigation was Ian Floyd, a detective with Scotland Yard, who was a member of the Special Projects Team. *Scotland Yard* (officially New *Scotland Yard*) is a metonym for the headquarters of the Metropolitan Police, the territorial police force responsible for policing all thirty-two boroughs of London, excluding the City of London. The Special Projects Team was made of fourteen experienced detectives who had a variety of skills that included surveillance, firearms, undercover, and finances. At the height of its activity, Anuric would employ more than fifty police officers.

Ian Floyd: "We knew Ruiz Henao was one of the big players, a major drug trafficker, the biggest Colombian drug trafficker operating in the United Kingdom of whom we knew. We identified him from intelligence in Colombia. I had to go to Colombia on three occasions to collect evidence. On the third occasion, we were at bank in Cali investigating when the Colombian police officers who were with us received word that criminal elements in Cali were aware of our presence and might do us harm. As the result of the threat, we were put in cars and taken back to our hotels. We were given armed guards and flown out of Cali and back to the United Kingdom the next morning. It didn't really harm our investigation. We had already collected most of our evidence. Later, I learned we had been under surveillance while in Colombia and they had photographs of us. But I didn't feel any danger while I was in Colombia. I felt we were well protected.

"In investigating the Colombians, we decided to target the money. It was a huge problem. They were making so much money because of the huge amount of drugs they were selling. We felt that the laundering of the money they sent back to Colombia could be their Achilles heel. It was really the first time in investigating drug trafficking that we targeted the money. We did it in two ways. Firstly, we tried to track the money back to the drug suppliers. Secondly, we tracked the money forward to try to identify the people in Colombia who would be receiving the money. In the end, we set up a joint investigation with the Colombians to target the suppliers of the drugs; that is, those who would have the money."

In the United Kingdom, financial institutions have a responsibility to report any suspicious activities. One of the suspicious activities was made by a company named TTT moneycorp, which was owned by Luis Fernando Carranza Reyes. There were also a couple of other suspicious activities involving money transfers.

When Carranza Reyes was arrested, he became a key witness, a supergrass, and an important link to Ruiz Henao because he was a money launderer for Ruiz Henao. Supergrass is a British slang term for an informant who turns Queen's evidence, often in return for protection and immunity from prosecution.

One of the major factors in Ruiz Henao's arrest was the evidence provided by Carranza Reyes. The authorities confiscated five million pounds, but according to Floyd, he had laundered perhaps five to ten times that amount. It took about a year before British authorities were ready to take Corranza Reyes to court. In 2004, he was sentenced to seven years in jail.

Corranza Reyes wasn't the only major Colombian drug trafficker taken down by British law enforcement.

Juan Evangelista Navarro Lopez was a principal target of Operation Alpington, which began in 2004. Lopez operated in Southeast London, while his handlers were based in Madrid, Spain.

Ian Munro is a detective sergeant with the Metropolitan Police who worked on Operation Alpington.

Ian Munro: "Lopez's job was to generate drug trafficking business with London organized crime for the Colombian cartel for which he worked. Tracking Lopez was very time consuming. We would get leads and spend a lot of time pursuing them, but you didn't know where they would lead, if anywhere.

"We reached a point in the investigation where we learned that Lopez had received a visit from two representatives of his handlers in Madrid. A drug deal had failed, resulting in the loss of a big drug shipment. The reps told Lopez he owed their bosses three million euros for the lost shipment. No way could Lopez re-pay that money, but he knew he was a dead man if he didn't. So he decided to flip and throw himself on the mercy of the British authorities. He literally walked into a police station and gave himself up."

The authorities turned Lopez into another supergrass informant.

Munro: "Lopez confirmed everything we knew, and he was willing to give evidence. Before Lopez, we had arrested twenty-five people and had twenty-two convictions with sentences totaling one hundred and six years. We were confident of adding to that total when we went to trial with Lopez. There were to be two trials. We were shocked when we lost the first trial. The jury just didn't believe Lopez, but we had to abide by its decision. We had done a good job professionally, and we deserved a better result. Because of the decision in the first trial, the prosecutors decided not to pursue a second trial."

Interestingly, one of the areas British investigators pursued was the identification of chemists employed by

Ruiz Henao and other Colombian drug traffickers. As British investigators became more successful in their investigations, Colombian traffickers were forced to become more sophisticated in how they got the drugs into the UK. Peter South, Detective Chief Inspector running the Metropolitan Police Service Special Projects Team, Operation Alpington, was one of those investigators.

Peter South: "The Colombians began to bring the drugs into the country imbedded in clothing, sawdust, and so forth. They needed chemists who could handle that kind of specialty. It required a lot of skill. So the chemists that were able to do that kind of work became extremely valuable to the drug traffickers. We were able to identify many of the chemists involved and arrested them. That caused major disruptions to their organizations."

Jesus had become totally aware that the police were doggedly on his tail, but he decided to travel with Gloria, his trusted associate, to Paris by road anyway.

Ruiz Henao: "I drove to Paris and didn't notice anyone following us. That night we went to a club. About half an hour later, a couple entered and took a seat next to us. They immediately started to talk to us and even offered to buy us drinks. I took Gloria to the dance floor, and while we were dancing, I told her that the couple seated next to our table, who were offering drinks to us, was not normal. We decided to leave the club and go to the hotel.

"As we were leaving, we stopped outside the street and started to chat for a few minutes. The couple that was inside the club came outside, and when they saw us, they didn't know what to do. They started to walk away. Gloria and I decided to return to the club. I ordered a bottle of Chivas Regal 21 whiskey, and we danced into night. Early in the morning, we went back to the hotel in central Paris to enjoy ourselves.

"Around 10 a.m., I switched my phone on, and immediately, I received a phone call from Tito, explaining to me that Fernando Carranza Reyes was arrested in London. Minutes later, my wife called to tell me the same thing. They were worried and thought that I was also arrested. I turned the TV on to see the news and saw the story about the British police operation that was done simultaneous in the United Kingdom, Spain, and Colombia, and that over thirty-four people were arrested.

"I immediately called my brother Jairo in Colombia. He was safe but unaware of what had happened. I then contacted all my associates in Colombia, and none of my people had been arrested. All the arrests were of Fernando's family and his workers, meaning that the British police were unaware of any of my contacts because none of them were arrested, not even my brother Jairo, who was dealing with Fernando's family in Colombia and collecting the money from them.

"At this stage, the British police were suspicious of me, but if none of my associates were arrested, I concluded it was because of a lack of evidence. After I contacted all my people and learned that everything was okay with all of us, I decided to return to London. In the afternoon, I drove Gloria to Charles de Gaulle Paris Airport, and she flew back to Madrid. I drove my Honda Civic from Paris to London through the English Channel by ferry."

As British pursued their investigation, Ruiz Henao was thinking long and hard about his future in the drug trade. In the summer of 2003, he decided to get out, figuring he had made enough money to retire.

Ruiz Henao: "After reflecting a long time, I decided to get out of the business. The police were on to me. I spoke to my boss Sergio in Colombia and my friends there, telling them that I was getting out because of the heat that was on me."

He paid off his closest associates and thanked them for working for him. He took a nice holiday in the Caribbean, and when he returned, he hoped to relax and enjoy his retirement.

"I made millions of pounds in the drug trade, but money had become less important to me. I had worked hard to make the money, but now the most important thing in my life was to spend time with my wife, son, and daughter. My pursuit of money cost me a good part of my life. Money can make you crazy and do stupid things. When I first started in the drug business, my goal was to make a million pounds, and I did. So l said to myself: 'I am going to carry on until I make ten million pounds.' I made that amount. At that point, I could buy a mansion, a yacht, pretty well anything, but I said to myself: 'Why stop now?' I then made fifty million pounds.

"At that point, I wanted to say to myself: 'Enough.' I had more money than I could ever possibly spend, and it was becoming a headache handling it. I could get out of the drug trade easily. I didn't have real enemies, so I could leave the drug trade and not be an easy target for anybody.

"I had no idea that Fernando Carranza Reyes had become a police informant, but I kept noticing that I was being followed by different cars. The next day, I called my brother-in-law Mario to meet me in a park near Baker Street. As we normally did when we traveled to a meeting point, we used public transportation.

"As Mario got off at the bus stop, a female brushed him and planted a microphone in his jacket. When we met, we started to walk around the park and talk about many things, unaware that the British police were watching and listening to everything we were doing. I said to Mario: 'Listen, Mario, at the end of the day, I don't worry about the millions of pounds we have lost. That's easy to recover. But the last thing I want to do is to go to prison.' Information from that conversation became one of the strongest pieces of evidence against me in court.

"After we were done talking, we went to a car dealership to buy a car. That's when we noticed a van with a lot of antennas following us. We immediately knew it was the police, so we went back to our homes.

"My boss and friends accepted my leaving the drug business, but some of my contacts in Spain started to put pressure on me, telling me that it was an excuse because I didn't want to work with them anymore. Some of them started threatening me, saying that they would do whatever necessary to get me killed. They warned me never to change telephone numbers or to leave them without any contact. They called me every day. The police managed to identify my numbers and intercept and record all the calls they made to me.

"I told Beto, Wilmar, and Tito that I was out of the business and to lose all contact with me because I was under police radar. Beto and Wilmar listened to me and stayed out of the cocaine business, but Tito continued in the business with a Spanish contact. One day, while he was meeting the Spaniard and unloading fifty kilos of cocaine from a lorry into his car, Tito was arrested. He was sentenced to fourteen years in prison. I was totally unaware of Tito's drug business at the time, but later it was all linked and used as evidence in my court case."

Jesus had stopped drug dealing. He felt he had exited at the right time. But then he made a stupid mistake.

"I couldn't resist it. I went by the office of a man named Fernando. We weren't really friends, but he was raving about the Mr. Big who controlled the local cocaine trade. Finally, I told Fernando I was the real Mr. Big. He got all excited. He nearly jumped out of the chair. He couldn't believe I was the real Mr. Big. He shook my hand. I shouldn't have opened my mouth, but I was proud what I had done. I let down my guard. It was stupid of me. I never saw Fernando again, and I hope I never see him.

"A couple of months later, Fernando was arrested. He told the police he knew who was behind the country's big cocaine trade. It was me. That was more evidence the police could use against me. My friends and associates were upset when I let that man know who I was. They said: 'Why the fuck did you do that and let him see your face?' I was too relaxed and over confident.

"I think that was the only reason they got me. I talked too much. Otherwise, they never would have caught me. After that, the police bugged my car and my home, and began to watch me. I would talk and talk in the car. I was too relaxed. I didn't realize the police were on to me. So I was talking, and they were recording it.

"The police didn't know who I was That's when I think they really started to investigate me. The police tried to say it was a four-year investigation, but that was a lie. It was more like four or five months. If they knew about me and let me traffic drugs into the United Kingdom, that would be criminal. During the four years, I brought thousands of kilos of cocaine into the United Kingdom. I was a threat to the wellbeing and health of the island.

"It didn't help me when my brother William was arrested. I began to be very careful in my drug dealings. At that point, some of my people were already arrested and in prison. For instance, my godmother, Mary Bolivar, was arrested and sentenced to life in prison. The police found evidence that pointed towards her being responsible for a contract killing in South London of a young Colombian man, nicknamed *Huevito*. He was strangled to death and found inside a car.

"None of the police evidence for that crime was related to me because the British police, I believe, were well aware that this was never my approach in this business. I was always against the use of violence. Sometimes I had to use threats to apply pressure, but I never took it to the extreme."

The police surveillance was becoming more intense, and it was unnerving Jesus. One evening, he went out with his family. When they returned, he noticed that the house alarm had been activated.

Ruiz Henao: "I entered the house very carefully while I told my family to wait outside. Upstairs in the master bedroom, I noticed that one door from the locker were open. I went outside and told my wife that it wasn't a burglar because nothing was missing. However, I was sure it was the police that had broken into my house.

"On another occasion, I went to meet my brother-in-law, Mario, and as we were travelling around London, we noticed a car with several antennas following us. I realized that the police were on to me, but I was happy to no longer be Mr. Big.

"I travelled to Madrid to speak to some of my friends and to work out what to do next. I went with my friend Gloria to meet an associate. We had a good discussion about the drug business. After the meeting, on our way back to Gloria's apartment, we noticed that we were being followed by a man. We got out of the car and walked to the middle of a street. Then we turned around and started to walk back towards the direction of the man. I just stared at him to see what he would do. The man did not know what to do. He looked confused and walked away. But when we walked to Gloria's apartment, he continued to follow us. We went back to the apartment and spent the night there. I knew that, if one tail went away, another would take its place.

"The next morning, I drove around Madrid. We went to a restaurant that was almost empty. The moment we ordered something to eat, two males entered the restaurant and took a table right in front of us. I told Gloria they were the police. We finished our meals. As soon as I paid the bill, we rushed out of the restaurant and hid around the corner. We saw the two men run out of the restaurant. They looked around for us, but we kept hidden until we saw them leave.

"While in Spain, I thought long and hard about fleeing to Brazil. They would never get me there. I could bring my family with me. I thought about the Great Train Robbery and how they managed to escape."

The Great Train Robbery was the robbery of £2.6 million from a Royal Mail train heading from Glasgow to London on the West Coast Main Line in the early hours of 8 August 1963, at Bridego Railway Bridge, Ledburn, near Mentmore in Buckinghamshire, England. Ronnie Biggs, one of the robbers, eventually fled to Brazil to avoid arrest. However, Jesus decided against going to Brazil.

"I flew to Colombia. Even though the police were watching me, I was confident that they had nothing on me. When I returned to the United Kingdom, I became more alert to things around me. I began seeing the authorities hanging around my home. One day, I was near my neighbors, an old couple, who were talking to a man. I said good morning to him. He replied good morning, but the old man got nervous and blurted out voluntarily that the man was the husband of his daughter.

"He wasn't very convincing. I knew that the man was really the police. I suspected the authorities were using my neighbor's house for surveillance. It was incredible. I don't know how the police could put an old couple like my neighbors in danger in a drug investigation. Luckily for them, we were not violent. I would see that old man and that police officer many times in my neighborhood. The old couple was not friendly with me anymore. When I left the house, I began to see a car following me.

"They bugged my car and my home, and I didn't have a clue. That is where I talked freely about the safe houses and my business, and that is where they got information about me. Before then, they didn't know anything about my safe houses. In the UK, the police can do anything they want. They can intercept calls and use the information for intelligence, but not in court.

"One day, I came home and found that the alarm was red. I thought somebody must have broken into my house. I suspected the police, but I couldn't find any evidence of it. Despite my suspicions, I didn't feel I had to change my routine. I couldn't do anything about it except go about my business as I normally did. I wasn't in the trade anymore. I was not doing anything criminal, so I felt I didn't have to change anything in my lifestyle. What could they possibly find out about me now that could hurt me in court?

"On another occasion, somebody broke into my car. I had parked the car in the same spot for ten years, and no one had touched the car. So why would somebody all of sudden try to break into my car? It had to be the police. I know they wanted me to know it was them who had broken into my car. They were playing psych games with me.

"I was in the bar one day where everybody was drinking beer except one guy who was drinking coffee and looking at me. I left the bar and the man followed me. But I managed to lose him. On another day, I was with Mario and I saw this car with three people cruising my neighborhood. We hid and waited until the car looked like it had left the neighborhood. We got out and started walking. Then the car came back again.

"Another day, I went to the chapel, and when I came out, I spotted someone in a car with tinted glass watching me. He lowered the window, and I could see these eyes staring at me. I talked about the police surveillance with a man from Medellín named John Lopez. He said not to worry about it. Lopez asked me if I could have a drink with him. He needed to talk to me. I met him in the bar and sure enough, I spotted the police tailing me.

"Lopez introduced me to an Indian man, who wanted to change one hundred thousand pounds into euros. Straight away I knew he was a cop. I told those around me to watch Lopez. He was an informant.

"The police were desperate trying to get evidence against me. They really wanted to put me away. The pressure that results from getting involved with drug trafficking is something you got to deal with every day. One wrong move and you end up in jail for several years. You wake up and say to yourself: 'Is this the day they catch me?' But now I was really starting to feel the pressure.

"The cloak-and-dagger game with the police was hard on my wife and kids. I was on edge, nervous, trying to figure out how I could get out of this mess with my freedom. It was my daughter's birthday. She was turning fifteen. She really wanted me to come to her birthday party. I had traveled to Brazil but made the decision to return home. 'Fuck it,' I told myself. 'I'm going to London.'

"They searched my luggage at the airport. I called my wife and told her I was back. She could sense something was wrong. I was on edge. She started crying and asked me what she could do to help me. I said nothing. She suggested that I fly back to Brazil. I said that I thought the police wouldn't let me the leave the country.

"I picked up my bag and took a train home. The police followed me from the airport. I was going crazy, thinking: 'What can I do? How can I escape?' But I knew there was nothing I could do. There was no escape.

"I don't know why they hadn't arrested me by now. I suspected that they had everything they needed on me. The only thing I can say is that they wanted to arrest me inside my home. They wanted to humiliate me in front of my family. I know it had an effect on my son. Until this day, he hates the police.

"On 17 November 2003, my wife drove me to Luton Airport, where I took a flight to Madrid. When I arrived, Gloria was waiting for me. I hugged her, and we started to walk towards a taxi when we noticed we were being followed. We got a taxi and went directly to a restaurant in central Madrid. We entered the restaurant and ordered some food. Again we saw two males and a female staring at us and trying to listen to our conversation.

"I mentioned to Gloria that it was strange because if the police had strong evidence against me, why would they let me leave the country? And we came to the conclusion that they must not have anything strong against me, and that's why I was being followed: to see if they could get something. So at this point I thought I was okay because I had been out of the drug business for over six months.

"On 23 November 2003, I flew back to London from Madrid and arrived to at Luton Airport. As soon as I got off the plane, I noticed many suspicious people around the airport terminal. I felt strange and knew the police were waiting for me. I walked to a phone box, called my wife, and told her that I arrived and that I saw them (the police) waiting for me. I got on a train to Central London and noticed the police around me. It's a strange feeling when you're being watched. My wife picked me up from Victoria train station, and we drove home. When we arrived, I explained to her what I had seen and that the police were on to me. With tears in her eyes, she told me to go run away, but I said that it would be impossible for me to do that because of the pressure that my contacts in Spain were putting on me about leaving the drug trade.

"The next day, I went to the bank trying to sort out money in my account. By now, I had cut off contact with anyone who was involved in my organization, especially the high up contacts in the United Kingdom. I also had cars that I had to get rid of and hide. I gave the cars away to associates who registered them under different names. I also gave associates some money that I had to get rid of. I never received the cars or money back. In prison, I found out that these people were arrested, and the cars and money were seized.

"I cleaned my house of any potential evidence, and I just stayed indoors thinking about what to do. I still believed the police did not have enough evidence on me because I was allowed to travel.

"I had a feeling the police would come for me, and it got stronger by the hour. Why they hadn't done it by now, I didn't know. I think it was probably to humiliate me. I checked with an Italian friend of mine and explained to him what was happening. He wanted to come to the house with guns to protect me. I was so desperate that I thought about it, but concluded it would be suicide.

"It was 27 November (2003), and I didn't want to leave home that night. I wanted to be with my family, but I needed money. So I went to the ATM. Again, the police followed me. It was depressing. At the time, I knew I didn't want to go to prison. I was thinking they would have to kill me if they came to arrest me.

"I called Mario to see how he was doing and explained the situation to him. Then I tried to get some sleep. At four o'clock in the morning, I heard a noise outside the house. I went to the bathroom, naked, and looked out the window. I saw the police jumping out of their cars. It was 27 November 2003…doomsday for me."

NINE

ARREST AND PROSECUTION

The game was up. The police had arrived at Jesus Ruiz Henao's home.

Ruiz Henao: "I was in bed with my wife when I heard noise coming from the outside. I instantly ran back to my wife and told her: 'They are here!' She was confused and asked: 'Who?' I said: 'The police.' I had some incriminating evidence, so I ran and picked up two SIM cards with very important information and a piece of paper with names and took them to the bathroom, naked, and flushed the information down the toilet.

"When I finished flushing, I heard the front door being smashed open and the house being flooded with police officers, at least a hundred of them, shouting: 'Police! Police!' There were about one hundred officers running into every room. I asked one of them near me to put a pillow over my hands so not to let my son see me in handcuffs, and he did it. Nevertheless, they were rude to my family, who were all crying.

"I had a hundred-year-old bottle of scotch, and the police drank it. They were drinking and cheering, looking full of happiness, as if they had just won the lottery."

Stephen Lear: "I was part of the arrest team. It was complicated. We had ten to fifteen addresses, and the raids had to be coordinated. We had about two hundred and fifty police involved in the takedown. It went smoothly, and we got everybody we wanted.

Ruiz Henao: "The police brought me downstairs. I was there for an hour before they took me by unmarked car to the Paddington Police Station. My sister-in-law, Maria, who was living with us at the time, was allowed to stay and take care of my two little ones."

Dozens of arrests were made in the autumn of 2003, mostly in London. Thirty-two people in the UK would admit to or be found guilty of criminal offenses relating to the Ruiz Henao investigation. In Colombia, seventeen more people were arrested and found guilty. In all, the total sentences across all of the investigations would add up to three hundred and fifty years. Authorities seized two tons of drugs, a quarter of which was cocaine; three-quarters ton of cannabis; and more than five million in cash assets.

Jesus was charged with conspiracy to supply Class A drugs as well as money laundering, Class A drugs in the UK include cocaine, crack cocaine, ecstasy (MDMA), heroin, LSD, magic mushrooms, methadone, and methamphetamine (crystal meth). Detective Superintendent Martin Molloy of the National Crime Squad talked to the press about the takedown's significance.

Martin Malloy: "We are looking at the possibility of the first one billion-pound drug cartel that we have ever dealt with. We believe we have ripped the heart out of drug trafficking in the UK."

Ruiz Henao: "I read in the newspapers that the price of a kilo of cocaine rose from twenty thousand to thirty thousand pounds within a week of my arrest. That's because my drug distribution network was pervasive. When we were busted, the supply dried up. We were the major suppliers for the big cities of Manchester, Liverpool, Glasgow, and Edinburgh. I would sell a kilo for twenty to twenty-three pounds, and it shot up thirty to thirty-five a kilo on the street. I actually felt good when I heard that. It showed that I was running my business properly."

Mario Tascon was also arrested and charged with supplying Class A drugs and for money laundering, but Jesus had been so low profile that the authorities confused their roles in the Ruiz Henao drug ring.

Ruiz Henao: "While I was in Spain, my brother-in-law, Mario, was contacted by *El Lincenciado*, our Spanish contact. He said he had one hundred kilos of cocaine in London and could get it to us for the very cheap price of eighteen thousand pounds per kilo. Mario, without my authorization, took the parcel and started to run the business again. The British police were watching him, and because of this, when we were busted, Mario was arrested as the number-one man in the organization, and I was arrested as the second-in-command."

Not everybody in the Ruiz Henao organization was captured. British police continued the hunt for Carlos Arturo Sanchez-Coronado, one of Ruiz Henao's principal money launderers, who had fled to Colombia. Sanchez-Coronado was captured and extradited back to the UK, where he admitted to three charges relating to money laundering and the use of fake passports.

Passing sentence at Southwark Crown Court, Judge Nicholas Loraine-Smith praised the efforts to extradite Sanchez-Coronado.

Judge Loraine-Smith: "I am delighted to see that cooperation between our two countries has resulted in this defendant facing his proper penalty. It shows that extradition is available not just for those at the top of criminal organizations but also for those much lower in it as well."

Sanchez-Coronado's sentencing meant prison terms totaling more than 253 years were imposed on Jesus's gang. The figure rose to well over three hundred and fifty when linked cases in Colombia were taken into account.

Although Sanchez-Coronado was considered a relatively minor player, his extradition was understood to have been personally backed by Colombia's vice president, Francisco Santos Calderon. The extradition represented a huge turnaround from the 1990s when the cartel's alleged links to government led to allegations of multimillion-dollar bribery. The success is being viewed as a template for the extradition of other drug fugitives from Colombia.

Ruiz Henao: "When I arrived at the police station, I was asked questions by the receiving officer in charge. What was my name, nationality, and if I was aware why I was arrested? They also questioned my family. In fact, they interviewed my wife for a couple of days. My wife told them she knew nothing. The police didn't believe her in the beginning, but later on, after interviewing me extensively, they realized she was telling the truth.

"At the beginning, my wife took my arrest very hard. She said: 'I didn't know you were involved with drugs. I didn't know you went with prostitutes. But because of the kids... Our daughter loves you... I am going to stick with you.' She did stick by my side and is still by my side. Today, the marriage is very good. She stuck with me all through the ordeal and never complained. Thankfully, nothing happened to her. Today, she is working and living a normal life.

"My daughter was also unaware of my criminal activities, but I had a talk with her. That was tough to do. She was so upset and crying all the time. She told me: 'I'm not going to blame you. I'm going to stick with you forever.' I thanked her. She stuck all the way with me and is still with me.

"My son was only about three years old, and he didn't really know what was going on. But what happened to me affected him. He would be sleeping, then, suddenly, he would jump up out of bed and start crying. He would try to destroy everything. He was feeling something, but at that age, he didn't know what it was. When he saw me in jail, he said he would kill all the guards and come home with me. I told him: 'Come on, you are only three years old. You don't know what you are talking about.' Later, when he became older, he said to me: 'Dad, I don't know everything that happened to you, but you are my dad and will always be my dad.'

"The authorities offered me the help of a solicitor. I was then taken to a cell where they took everything from me and locked me in. I dropped myself onto the hard cement bed and covered my face, not wanting to see anything. The only thing I could think of was my daughter, my son, and my wife. My mind was in complete chaos. I could not think properly, and I was shaking the whole time.

"Sometime later, the door opened and I was offered some water. I asked to see a lawyer that I knew: Nigel Dean from Edward Fail and Waterson solicitors. I was told that they were trying to get in touch with him. I was later told that Mr. Dean was not available, but someone on his behalf had arrived and was waiting in the interview room. There was myself, two officers, and the lady acting as my solicitor. The lady lawyer was introduced to me, but we were not allowed to speak.

"They said my interrogation was one of the longest ever… six or seven days. There were four interrogations my first day of arrest, all of them were about two or three hours. An interview would start, and I was read my rights.

"In the evening, I was taken back to my cell and I sat in a corner with my head between my legs, wanting to finish everything at that moment. I didn't sleep, the night was so long. I had no idea at what time the cell doors would open again, and I would be taken for more interviews. The next day, I was not allowed to shower and clean up. I was once again taken to the interview room where I was asked hundreds and hundreds of questions. My answer never changed. It was 'no comment.' I had about five interviews that day, but, at that point, I still didn't believe they had enough strong evidence against me.

"When they started asking me questions I wanted to answer, the prosecution gave me a choice. Do you want to answer the questions or not? If you do, I will help you answer them. But you have the right as well to no comment. It wasn't hard to answer the questions: Where do you live? Where were you born? But I worried that if I answered, I would get in trouble. So I didn't answer a single question.

"They began an interview by asking me my name. I was bombarded with hundreds of questions and I replied the same to all of them: 'no comment.' I answered the questions, but then I was advised by my solicitor not to answer any more questions. After an interview, I was returned to my cell where I immersed myself in deep sorrow. I have a vague memory of that day.

"Later, I was taken to the interview room again and asked hundreds of questions. All of them were basically the same questions, but asked differently, Again, I answered the questions with 'no comment.' After the second interview, I noticed that the evidence was not strong against me, but what I didn't realize was that the interviewing officer was leaving the strongest evidence till last.

"They did the old cop trick. One interrogator was a good cop; the other a bad cop. One was polite and the other was real aggressive. It's just like in the movies. The polite one acted like he wanted to be my friend. The more aggressive cop acted like he was my worst enemy. It was planned. It's not just the UK police who act that that way. Anywhere you go in the world, cops act like that. When I see the good cop, bad cop routine in the movies or on TV, I have to laugh."

The police interviewed Jesus at the Charing Cross police station on 30 November 2003. Here is a part of one of the police interviews.

Interrogator: 8th August 2000. Five thousand pounds of deposited cash into that bank account. One day, another five thousand pounds. Another day, three thousand cash. Another five days later, six thousand pounds cash; another day later,

6,040 pounds And then on the 21st of that month, that is, the 21st of August, four thousand pounds cash... the 25th of August, one thousand pounds cash. Nice sums accumulate there, which took your balance to 30,548.52 pounds. Where has that come from?

Ruiz Henao: No comment.

Interrogator: What is the source of those deposits?

Ruiz Henao: No comment.

Interrogator: Which company has employed you and paid you cash?

Ruiz Henao: No comment.

Interrogator: You obviously got vast amounts of money in hand. And then on the 25th of August there is a transfer of thirty thousand pounds. So, Mr. Ruiz Henao, who made that transfer?

Ruiz Henao: No comment.

Interrogator: Okay. Did you authorize the transfer?

Ruiz Henao: No comment.

Interrogator: Where did the transfer go?

Ruiz Henao: No comment.

At that point the interview ended.

Ruiz Henao: "I was taken to the magistrate court because the police needed to ask for permission to extend the time for more interviews. At the magistrate court, I saw my brother-in-law, Mario; his wife, my sister, Omaira; and my wife Maria. That's when I realized they were also arrested. I nearly feel on my knees. It was my worst nightmare to see my wife and family there. I thought about my son and daughter without their mother, and I cried in silence.

"It was hard for me to breathe. An officer noticed me and offered me some water. The time extension for interrogation was granted by the judge, and I was taken back to the police station.

"Later that day, I was taken to another interview, and this time more pressure was put on me by the interviewing officer, as they disclosed information about my wife. They said she was in a police cell, and there was the possibility of her getting a prison sentence. I stood my ground and continued to answer all the questions with a dry 'no comment.'

"But seeing my wife detained in the police station made me angry, and I began to be very rude with the police and even with my counsel. The police were totally aware that she had no idea of what was going on. They were listening in to all my conversations and watching us 24/7. Why was she arrested? Who knows? If the police had done a proper investigation, they would have known that she had no idea of my business and was never involved.

"The interview time was extended for five days. It was the longest time ever for a drug conspiracy case. After two days, when the police didn't get any answers from me, my wife and my sister were released without any charges. The police only arrested them to try and use the arrest against me and to get something out of me.

"On the fifth day of my being held by the police, Mario, Beto, Wilmar, and I were taken to court. This time, we got charged with money laundering and conspiracy to traffic in drugs. The police also made an application to the judge to place us in the highest risk prison because the police stated that I could just click my fingers and people around the world would die. I was a very dangerous leader, the authorities maintained, with the capacity and intelligence to get a conspiracy running in minutes. To them, I had the power and money to pay for anything and to bribe anyone. I could get members of my organization to break me out of prison. I just stood quietly and listened to the nonsense. Meanwhile, the judge believed the prosecution and sent us to the highest security prison in the United Kingdom.

"When I was busted, I had £220,000 in the bank. About eighty thousand pounds of that amount was legitimate. It was the winnings from the spot the ball contest. They took that money away from me, claiming it was drug sale earnings. They also took our house, cars, and everything we owned. They really couldn't take our house. Our family home belonged half to my wife and twenty-five percent to my children. Only twenty-five percent of the house was mine.

"The home was in my wife's name, but the authorities sold the house and gave my family provisional accommodation. My wife paid cheap rent, sixty pounds a week for a one-bedroom flat. It wasn't right, though, that they took my house. I got a solicitor. It took about six years, but I finally won in court. They had already sold the house, so the police had to give my wife £120,000 in compensation.

"The police closed down the restaurants I owned, and the government confiscated them. They took everything. It totaled £55.4 million and included our cars and property. They found a lot of money in two stash houses and in the bank, but they found only five thousand pounds in my home.

"I already paid everybody off in Colombia, so I was the only one who lost money. I gave one man two to three million euros to hold for me. But then I got arrested. I thought the man would hold the money for me until I got out. A couple of years later, that man was murdered, and I was out all that money.

"I pled guilty to the charges. Should I have fought it? I felt I could beat the drug trafficking conspiracy charge, but there was no chance against the money laundering charge. I had spent a lot of money, but I didn't have the income to support that spending. They offered me a deal. I discussed it with my solicitor, Nigel Dean. He suggested I plead guilty."

Jesus went to court every three months for about two years. He was incarcerated in Belmont, a high-security prison, but moved to Belmarsh, another high security prison. Belmarsh is a Category A men's prison located in Thamesmead, Southeast London. Category A prisons are high-security prisons that house male prisoners who, if they were to escape, would pose the most threat to the public, the police, or national security. It is run by Her Majesty's Prison Service.

"I was the first ever Latino person to enter into a United Kingdom prison as a double A high-risk prisoner. I had to be escorted by ten officers in an unmarked, blacked-out truck and a police helicopter following the truck. We didn't stop anywhere, not even for traffic lights. I was moved to the unit in Belmarsh prison as a remand prisoner pending my court case.

"I was put in isolation. I was in Belmarsh for about two and a half years before they moved me to Woodhill prison. I was there for another two and a half years in isolation. They considered me a very dangerous criminal, with a number of powerful connections. The law figured I could make a conspiracy very easy. As I said, the police said, literally, with a flick of the finger, I could make people disappear, and the judge believed it.

"I was taken to Southwark Crown Court in Southwest London, which was presided by Judge Loraine-Smith and the Criminal Prosecution Service (CPS). The court presented the preliminary charges. The judge asked me how I wanted to plead. I said: 'not guilty.' The charges stated that I was the head of a United Kingdom organization involved in conspiracy to traffic in cocaine and money laundering, worth a billion pounds. They tried to charge me with trafficking in heroin and marijuana, but I never touched those drugs.

"After many days in Crown Court, a date for my trial was fixed for September 2004. We spent five months preparing my case. My solicitor, Nigel Dean, came to see me every day. It was very hard work. I was certain that I would have to go to trial.

"The prosecution tried to convince Mario to testify against me, but he stood his ground and declined their offer. They made a deal with Beto and Wilmar in which they agreed that, in return for testimony against me, they would serve just four years in prison.

"As the trial date came closer, the prosecution tried to put pressure on me to admit my guilt. They offered me some benefits: twenty-five percent reduction in my sentence. They would keep my assets they had confiscated already, but there would be no charges for any hidden assets. My defense considered this offer carefully. I didn't want to go to trial, but I rejected the offer. I concluded it would be impossible to fight the money laundering charge. I was tied to millions. How could my defense explain the millions of pounds connected to me?

"As for the drug trafficking conspiracy charge, I was sure I would beat it. The evidence wasn't strong enough. To make a case, they had to convince some of my associates to testify against me. Would the court believe them? I had my doubts.

"I thought I would fight the case and even go to court. There was a lot of legal wrangling between my lawyers and the court, but then the prosecution came to me with a proposition. Plead guilty, and the judge would take one-third my sentence off. I was offered twenty-five years. So that meant I would get seventeen years. I took the deal. But they actually gave me nineteen years. Later, I appealed the sentence and won."

About two months after his arrest, he got some bad news. His brother, Jairo, was murdered. Nicknamed the Mouse, Jairo worked at a tomato wholesaler, selling to storekeepers in a marketplace. He was described as hard working. Witnesses told the police that they didn't know of anyone who would want to kill him.

Around 4:50 p.m., a dark-colored RX or AX motorbike arrived with two people on it. One of them stayed on the bike, and the other went into the street. There were gunshots, according to witnesses, and Jairo was dead, wounded in the heart. A ten thousand dollar note was found on Jairo's body.

Ruiz Henao: "Some of the people who used to work for me in Colombia took my house after my arrest. They had turned against me. Jairo's death was a warning to me: Don't open my mouth. Of course I would never open my mouth. I vowed that I would get whoever killed Jairo when I got out of prison. Later, I learned that the killer was Diego Bahos. He was murdered by a very powerful person."

Jesus looked for help with his case from wherever he could find it. One of the individuals who tried to help was Jeremy Corbyn, a prominent British politician who would serve as leader of the Labor Party and leader of the opposition from 2015-20. When Jesus met him, he had been a member of parliament (MP) for Islington North since 1983. Ideologically, Corbyn identifies as a socialist and democratic socialist.

Ruiz Henao: "I came to know Jeremy Corbyn in late 1987. I went to meet him at his office in the community. We were living in his neighborhood he represented. We became good friends. I went there with my wife and daughter, who was months old. For me, he was a very good man, very helpful and very conscientious.

"At that point, I was not doing anything with drugs. I approached him about the possibility of getting a British passport. He was attentive. Later, in some way, I think he was aware of my being involved with drugs. He really didn't want to know too much. We talked by phone. He asked me if I was involved with drugs. I said yes, but not directly. He said he would try to help me. He wrote letters to the police in 2003. My last communication with Corbyn was in 2013 when my daughter sent him a letter requesting his help in finding a human rights organization that could help with my case.

"My daughter explained in the letter: 'my father has no legal representation, and (he) has been through a whole trial without it and no Spanish interpreter. We have no one else that can help us, not even a lawyer, as the judge has denied my father from having legal aid.' Corbyn replied, saying he couldn't really help because we were now living in a different area. That was just before he became leader of the Labor Party. When he became leader, we lost contact. But I liked him."

As Jesus awaited sentencing, he lost contact with everyone in his past life except his wife and family. On 12 May 2005, Jesus and Mario Tascon stood before Judge Loraine-Smith for sentencing. Here is part of what the judge said.

"The people who really run the drug industry in this country are very rarely caught and sentenced. This is because they pay other people to carry out the dangerous work where an arrest is more likely. Their fingerprints are not found on the drug packaging. No telephone of theirs is shown to have made relevant calls. Nothing incriminating is found in their home. Others carry out their tasks. Meanwhile, they make enormous profits from this foul trade.

"An extensive and lengthy investigation produced a compelling case against you, Ruiz Henao and Mario Tascon, and to one in which you pleaded guilty, albeit on a limited basis, which I will strictly adhere to. It was suggested that those pleas should gain maximum credit. That cannot be right and would be unfair to those who immediately admit offense and plead at the first available opportunity…. I agree your basis of plea certainly recues the term, and as I have said, I have taken a number of matters into account, most obviously your plea."

The judge then sentenced Jesus to nineteen years imprisonment concurrent with ten years given on count two, for a total of nineteen years. A concurrent sentence of ten years was also imposed for the offense of assisting to retain the proceeds for drug trafficking. The court noted that the police had seized five hundred and fifty kilos of cocaine, which had been directly linked directly or indirectly to Jesus's organization.

Tascon was given seventeen years imprisonment on count one to be served concurrently with the ten years passed on count two, the money laundering charge. The judge also recommended Jesus and Tascon for deportation. Unless the parole board recommended otherwise, they would have to serve at least two-thirds of their sentences.

Others members were convicted. Jesus's brother, William, was jailed for sixteen years; Ramon Navarro got eighteen years; Roque Garcia Martinez, thirteen years; Ivan Garcia Ospina, sixteen years; and Wilmar de Jesus Ospina and Juan Rojes-Pineda, four years.

The takedown of Jesus's criminal operation was impressive. In the last two years, authorities had seized £2.5 million in cash and two tons of drugs worth an estimated £100 million in street sales.

The press was not allowed to report on the case while it was being prosecuted, but once Jesus and his gang were convicted, a flood of press articles appeared. The press reported how a Colombian "refugee" had come to the UK and established the biggest cocaine organization in the island's history. The *Daily Mirror* reported about how "they seemed to be quiet, respectable bus drivers and cleaners, but in reality they masterminded a billion-pound drug gang." The *Times* reported that "the wholesale price of a kilo of cocaine in the underworld rapidly rose from twenty thousand pounds to thirty thousand pounds after the arrests three years ago and has only recently started to fall." The *Daily Mail* described Jesus as "unobtrusive and low key" and a "church-going mastermind."

Top crime officials commented to the press about the convictions.

Detective Superintendent of the National Crime Squad Mark Malloy said, "We are looking at the first billion-pound drug cartel we have ever dealt with."

Tariq Ghaffur, Assistant Commissioner in Charge of Scotland Yard's drug investigations, commented, "A criminal business saw a market place in London, dipped their toe in, and went on from there."

Deputy Chief Superintendent of the Metropolitan Police Sharon Kerr stated, "We have seen nothing like this before. The case dispels the myth that drug smugglers are violent gangsters. These men were not violent. They led normal, middle-class lives."

TEN

BEHIND BARS

Jesus Ruiz Henao's living space for the next several years would be a dismal and cramped six-by-nine prison cell. When he entered prison, Jesus was considered a highly dangerous inmate, and he was put in high security away from the general population. He spent the first two and a half years in Belmont Station and another three and a half years in HM Prison Woodhill, a Category A male prison, located in Milton Keynes, England. Jesus's isolation during those six years made his cell seem like a prison inside of a prison. After six years, Jesus was finally moved into the general population.

Ruiz Henao: "The first day in prison was horrible. I laid on my bunk with the pillow over my head. I was depressed and wanted to kill myself, but they were watching me twenty-four hours, around the clock. It was impossible to commit suicide. My daughter came to the prison. She cried when she heard me talk about suicide. She said: 'Do it for me. Stay alive!' I listened to her.

"At first I missed everything: the money, the food, the ability to walk around at leisure. But as the months and years went by, I came to miss my wife and children above everything. The most important thing for me in prison was to make a phone call to my wife and family and ask: 'How are you?' Contact with my family helped to keep me sane. To know that my family was all right meant everything to me. My family was my life. My wife was there for me 24/7. My wife and children gave me the hope and strength to endure prison. I wanted to talk to them every single day, but I was not allowed to do that.

"I saw prisoners who had lost family contact. They just didn't seem to care about living anymore.

"Life in prison was incredibly boring. You didn't have human contact with anyone. Typically, I woke up at 7 a.m. with nothing to do. There were no programs for the inmates, nothing. About eleven o'clock they gave us lunch. At 3 or 4 p.m., we had about forty-five minutes to take a shower or to make a telephone call. Then it was back to the cell. The food was horrible—pies, mashed potatoes, starchy food—and it was not good for you.

"There were very dangerous people in my unit. Gary Vinter, a stone-cold killer, was in for triple murder. He kept saying that if he got close to someone, he was going to kill them. He kept telling anyone who would listen: 'I'm going to die in prison. There is nothing they can do to me. I'm serving life without parole.' He made me nervous.

"Another prisoner, named Tyson, mid-thirties, was a very good man. I got along well with him. He would protect me from the guards who tried to take advantage and control of not just me but other prisoners. He told them: 'If anyone touches my friend, I will kill the motherfucker.'

"One time, I wanted to go to the shower. Tyson said thoughtfully: 'Don't go in the shower without shoes.' He tossed me a pair of slippers. One day, some of the inmates wouldn't let me use a phone, and he told them: 'Let him use a phone.' Tyson is a very good man but don't ever try to cross him.

"The other prisoners came to know who I was and what I had done in the drug trade. They had a lot of respect for me. I garnered a reputation in prison as being Mr. Big. If a Colombian prisoner wanted to do something, he came to me. I was like the boss.

"Being respected meant that I was protected. Still, a couple of times I had to stand my ground. On one occasion, I went to do some laundry in the laundry room when an Iranian man, who was in charge of the laundry room, began to throw my clothes out of the washing machine and on to the floor. He yelled at me and said that I couldn't wash my clothes. I immediately went to another Colombian prisoner, who worked in the kitchen, and asked him to let me borrow two small knives. He had the knives hidden in his cell and had stolen them while working.

"He gave me the knives, and I hid them under my shirt and returned to the laundry room. When I arrived, I threw a knife to the Iranian man and held the other one. I told him: 'Come on, you have a knife. I have a knife. Let's go to the shower. Only one of us will come out alive and stay in this prison forever!' The other inmates who were in the laundry room began to leave. The Iranian man started to shout, trying to get the attention of the guards; I grabbed the knives and hid them under a washing machine. Then I ordered the Iranian to 'leave the fucking room!' He immediately left, and I put my clothes to wash. From that point on, the Iranian man always kept quiet when I went to do my laundry.

"There are a lot of Muslims in British prisons. I think they make up about seventy percent of the prison population. Many of them get radicalized in prison. I believe British prisons create terrorists, or at least the conditions for terrorism.

"Of course, Muslims don't celebrate Christmas. In fact, you couldn't say Christmas in prison. You had to say holiday season. I hate that because if you are expected to respect the Muslim faith, they need to respect the faiths of others, including Christianity. Some Muslims tried to convert me. They even brought me a Spanish Koran, but I stalled them, saying: 'Let me think about it.'

"I went to a Muslim man who had dealt drugs with me and was doing thirty years for murder. He was very powerful in the Muslim prison community. He was in a different prison, so I had to get a mobile phone to call and let him know how I was being forced to become a Muslim. He talked to the Muslims who were trying to convert me. He told them: 'Listen, I am Jesus's brother. You cannot force him to do anything he doesn't want to do. He respects us. We need to respect him.' It worked. Otherwise, I would have had to become a Muslim.

"Unlike in America, the British prisons do nothing to rehabilitate inmates. You can be a good person, but you won't have any time deducted from your sentence. Ninety percent of British inmates who get out end up re-offending. They don't have any programs for the inmates in some of the prisons in which I was incarcerated. You work in prison, but that's not really rehabilitation. You can become a better criminal in prison than you were before you came in. Most people who come to prison will do crime again once they are released. Prison is a school for crime.

"In prison, there is lots of corruption. The guards will get you anything you need for a price. You can get anything you can get in normal life—weapons, drugs, a cell phone. Outside of getting a cell phone, I didn't take advantage of the corruption.

"I saw a lot of violence and a lot of people die. One time, there was a water leak on the landing. An inmate was upset about it. There were these three young prisoners who didn't like him. He blamed the young prisoners for the leaking problem. After arguing, they all went back to their cells. The next morning, a guard came to the man's door and opened it. The three young boys rushed into the man's cell and stabbed him to death.

"Homosexuality is really not common in British prisons. I believe homosexuality is a middle-to-upper class phenomenon. It is rare to see a middle-to-upper class person in a British prison. Most of the prisoners are lower class, and they don't like homosexuality. Actually, homosexuality is more common among the Muslim men. I was propositioned by a Muslim in prison, but I told him I don't go for that type of thing. He left me alone.

"I made a lot of friends, some of them with whom I'm still in contact. I believe many of the inmates in British prisons are innocent. I knew one prison inmate friend who was serving twenty-four years. He and a couple of friends got into a fight with a patron at a bar. They beat the patron up badly, nearly killed him. His uncle went to pick him up. He was seen on a camera and charged with being an accessory to a crime. He's doing time in prison."

By the end of 2007, Jesus was transferred to HMP Lowdham Grange prison, a Category B training prison situated in Nottingham and operated by Serco, a company that primarily derives its income as a contractor providing government services. Lowdham Grange houses adult male offenders aged twenty-one and over with sentences over four years and with at least twelve months to serve. It has a maximum capacity of nine hundred and twenty inmates.

Ruiz Henao: "It was a good prison. I was allowed to associate and be with other prisoners. It was here that I started taking courses, such as sociology, computers, and marketing, to pass the time.

"I met fellow Colombians in the prison who knew other British inmates involved in the drug business. They all wanted to try to distribute cocaine from inside the prison. I would get involved, but that turned out to be a big mistake.

"In the prison, I met a group of English inmates that were looking for a contact person to supply cocaine. I was introduced to them by a Colombian named Martin, who was serving fifteen years for cocaine conspiracy. One of the Brits I met was Russell Knaggs, a hardened prisoner in his late thirties, who was spending sixteen years in prison on drug offenses. He was very charismatic, and I liked him.

"We started talking and planning how to get back into the cocaine trade in the future. He asked me to be his drug supplier. I was scheduled to get out in May 2012, but I had no money. The money from a drug deal would give me a stake for my future. I agreed to work with him.

"I was given a mobile phone and started to call some old friends on the outside again. For many months, the Brits and I had many meetings inside the prison about the drug conspiracy we were hatching. After a few months, I managed to get in contact with my old boss Sergio in Colombia. I spoke to him through the mobile phone about potentially supplying three hundred kilos of cocaine from South America to this group of English men headed by Knaggs. After a few conversations with Sergio, he agreed to do it, even though he did not know these men. He trusted me one hundred percent. His associate Diego would be his point man in the drug deal.

"We arranged for me to meet Duberly Naevez-Alvarez, a naturalized British citizen of Colombian descent. He visited me in prison, and we talked about a possible drug deal.

"Duberly had met an English man outside named Peter Hadley, who had been involved in a drug seizure in Rotterdam, Holland, and, unknown to him, was now under police surveillance. The British police saw Duberly meeting Hadley and they began to tail Duberly. The police learned that Duberly was going to visit me.

"I warned Duberly about meeting with Hadley. He didn't know anything about him. The police were on to Hadley, maybe watching him. I was right.

"The police bugged our conversation and recorded everything. They heard me tell Duberly to meet Diego, my contact in Colombia, and speak with him about the possibility of arranging a drug parcel that could be delivered to mainland Europe. Duberly agreed to meet Diego. The British police were now hot on our tail, and I came under investigation as part of a conspiracy to import cocaine from inside a prison.

"Duberly did what I told him to do. He travelled to Cali, Colombia, and met with my contact, Diego. It was a productive meeting. Diego agreed to source the three hundred kilos of cocaine that would be delivered to mainland Europe. I contacted Diego from my mobile phone inside the prison where he informed me of the decision. I thanked Diego. He said that because I had vouched for Duberly, he would do the deal without hesitation.

"Martin kept my mobile phone hidden inside the prison. He would be the link between me and the other conspirators inside the prison."

The plot involved arranging for the drugs to be shipped from Colombia to Europe hidden in consignments of fruit. The drugs would arrive to the drug traffickers via Costa Rica, California, Germany, and Belgium. Hadley would be in charge of providing money and arranging contacts, including travel to South America.

The men communicated in code, referring to the plot as "a plastering job." Knaggs, using the pseudonym George, would oversee the plan. In addition to Ruiz Henao and Hadley (codenamed Mike), Knaggs recruited some other people. Robert Rich, referred to by the pseudonyms Vince and Elvis, was responsible for direct contact with Knaggs, meeting external contacts, attending meetings, and being on the ground in South America, which he visited on three occasions.

Duberly, referred to by the pseudonym Jose, had been instructed by Ruiz Henao to facilitate the sourcing of the drugs in Colombia, to where he travelled for that purpose. Anthony Perger's role was to assist with transportation and warehousing. His pseudonym was Tony. The gang referred to the drugs in conversations and messages as "oil," "plastering job," "cigarettes," "motorbike," and "cars."

Ruiz Henao: "About two weeks after my first meeting with Duberly, he came to visit me again at prison with my brother, Hector. We spoke all about his travel and how Diego had agreed to do the deal. Once again, the British police bugged and recorded the entire conversation. It later became evidence in court.

"I was totally unaware that Russell Knaggs, from inside the prison, and Peter Hadley, on the outside, were in contact by an illegal mobile phone and that they planned to import the cocaine into the UK after it arrived into mainland Europe. They also spoke about selling a motorcycle for five thousand pounds. The police would later use that as evidence, determining that the term 'motorcycle' was code for drugs, and that the conspirators planned to import five thousand kilos. But the man who was selling the motorcycle had nothing to do with any drug deal.

"Dates were set, and Diego was ready to source the three hundred kilos of cocaine. However, I was unaware that Diego got into a fight in Colombia with a very powerful group. One afternoon in April 2010, in Pereira, Colombia, while he was having some drinks with his nephew and a friend in a bar, Diego was gunned down by two people with machine guns. Diego and his friend died immediately, and his nephew was rushed to hospital in critical condition, but he died two days later. When I learned the news, I told Russell Knaggs that the deal was off because Diego was murdered, and I couldn't find a new cocaine source. So we called it off."

On 17 September 2008, however, during a search of Michael Phillips' cell, a document written by Knaggs and Phillips, and with the latter's fingerprints on it, was found. The authorities determined it was a blueprint for the importation of tons of cocaine from South America into the UK via Spain. The document contained references to quantities of fruit; to the chances of encountering and avoiding x-ray; to Rich (Vince) meeting up with someone in

Spain; and to the aim of moving as much product as possible in a three-month window.

On 8 March 2009, Hadley visited Knaggs at the prison, and a covert recording of their conversation, parts of which were inaudible, was made. With the assistance of a senior lecturer in phonetics, the authorities determined the recording showed that Hadley and Knaggs had talked in considerable detail about the importation in containers of large quantities of drugs from Costa Rica to the UK via Florida, Hamburg, and Belgium, and how they would make large amounts of money from the transaction.

In the conversation, Knaggs told Hadley: *"At the end of six months, you and I would have had a million – a million on top of ten million... three thousand euros plus. We've got to pay fifteen hundred dollars to move it into Costa Rica... the way it's going to be done is if it's going to be vacuum packed... the only thing that is going to trip us up is information received..."*

The plan continued, as Duberly, Rich, and Hadley on the outside kept trying to consummate a deal. There was travel, meetings, emails, and telephone conversations.

On 14 May 2009, a Yahoo! email account, slimjim25@ymail.com, was created in Cali, Colombia, by Rich and Duberly using the name James Smith for the account holder. As part of the operation, a collaborator in Colombia would log into the email account and write a draft email. An accomplice based in Europe would then read the message, delete it from both the draft and trash folders and write his own draft so as to not leave behind any messages that could be read by law enforcement.

They would use the Yahoo! account to discuss the new deal and its details (dates, containers and quantities). Every time they wrote a message, the receiver would delete it. Unknown to Knaggs and his collaborators, Yahoo! received requests from United Kingdom police and the FBI in September 2009 and April 2010 to preserve all the emails.

In response, Yahoo! created several "snapshots" of the email account to preserve the content at the time and to reveal the messages. Yahoo! managed to recover all the deleted emails. Later, they were used as the main evidence in court against all of the defendants, and it secured their convictions.

Russell Knaggs managed to take the Yahoo! representatives in America to court to explain how they managed to recover a deleted email from a server, something that seemed physically impossible to do. Yahoo!'s explanation was unsatisfactory.

The prosecution later charged that the account was used from that day onwards by Rich, Hadley, and, on occasion, Alvarez, to communicate with each other securely from different locations. They did this by variously logging into the account (using the password *americano69*) and creating, reading, or altering draft emails. This would avoid interception and the need to send the email. In this communication, George (Knags) was often referred to as G; Vince (Rich) as V; Jose (Alvarez) as J or H; and Tony (Berger) as T.

On the day that the email account was opened, Rich drafted an email to Hadley saying: *"Hi mate, the bank is Barclays account no. 00025526 sort code. 20-21-78 Miss Monica motto is it possible to put another 500 into it will you speak to George??? Cheers pal, take care."*

On 15 May 2009, Hadley drafted a reply to Rich, saying: *"Got it ok mate did h wife get the 500 I sent the name was m c London, g said this guy is sending part of the oil with h yet i heard h say he did not know the name! what the fuck is going on mate I'm not handing any more over until I know who is who and what part they play i have to cash t up so he can visit try and find out mate g not making me good all these people involved but they don't have cash! g saying h putting oil on and someone else and the guy whose wife's a/c I put the cash in that's 3, g says londono is h mate and made the intro to h so he's putting 50 barrels on, this other guy 100 and h 150!!!"*

On 20 June 2009, following a telephone call between Rich and Duberly, Ruiz Henao was visited at HMP Lowdham Grange by his brother, Hector, and Duberly. They spoke in Colombian Spanish and talked in what was said to be highly incriminating detail about the need to be wary of surveillance, shipments in containers, a delivery in a month's time followed by one every two months, buying goods, the transportation fee, the cost of bribing a corrupt official, sums of money in euros and US dollars, and the need to build up capital. The conversation was recorded by the authorities and translated from Spanish to English.

On 7 August 2009, a meeting was held between Hadley, Rich, Alvarez, Hector, and two of Alvarez's cousins at a public house situated about a mile from HMP Lowdham Grange. Alvarez and Hector then visited Ruiz Henao, and they discussed Hadley and Rich's forthcoming trip to South America and the funding of any transaction that would result.

The prosecution later alleged at trial that Ruiz Henao gave instructions to put pressure on Knaggs so that matters could progress, and that Ruiz Henao also spoke to Hadley about getting cash for travel expenses. After the visit, Hector and Alvarez returned to the public house where Hadley, Rich, and the others had waited, and a further discussion took place between them. The conversation, which was partly recorded by the authorities, included reference by Hadley to travelling himself and "six thousand each." Rich referred to many people being involved and the need to get "it done by September."

The calls, emails, and meetings continued into the fall of 2009. The Knaggs' group was still unaware that the authorities were monitoring them. On 7 November 2009, Alvarez was arrested taking delivery of 2.6 kilos of cocaine in Paris.

Four days later, the police searched the cells of Knaggs and Ruiz Henao. Incriminating evidence was found. A piece of paper recovered from Knaggs' cell contained details of addresses in Colombia, a contact number in Colombia "to leave messages," and details in relation to Ruiz Henao and Hector, with a London number and the instruction to "leave a message."

A diary found in Knaggs' cell contained Hadley's address and his partner's email address. A piece of paper was found in Ruiz Henao's cell, which allegedly listed properties owned by Knaggs and his relatives, which were intended to be sold to raise money for the purchase of drugs in Colombia.

On the same day, a search was carried out at Hadley's address. A laptop computer was recovered, examination of which revealed that it had been used to log on to the *slimjim* account. Drafts and fragments of draft email communications on that account were also found on the laptop. During a search at Rich's address, a computer tower was found which, examination subsequently showed, had also been used to log on to the *slimjim* account.

On 21 November 2009, during a prison visit by his wife and children, Ruiz Henao was recorded discussing in detail the failure of the operation. He talked about his suspicion that the operation had been infiltrated, the arrest of Alvarez in Paris, and the prospect of a successful prosecution of those involved. The investigation continued into early 2010, when the authorities decided they were ready to take down the plot.

Ruiz Henao: "On a gloomy day in May 2010, at five in the morning, I was suddenly awakened by the sound of the British police opening my cell door in Lowdham Grange prison. I was in bed when they turned the lights on. They told me to get dressed. I was once again under arrest for conspiracy to import cocaine into the UK.

"I was handcuffed and taken out of my prison cell. When I looked around, I saw hundreds of police officers and noticed that other inmates were being arrested. Russell Knaggs, Martin Gordillo, Koubary, and me were moved to the isolation unit, and our cells were totally emptied by the police. They took everything from the cells and did a full search, item by item. They managed to find the mobile phone that I was using, inside Martin's cell.

"As the police started their interview with Martin, he panicked and told them that he wanted to speak but was afraid for himself and his family. He told the authorities everything. He explained that he was forced to hide the mobile phone for very powerful and dangerous people. The police didn't charge him in our drug conspiracy.

"I was interviewed for several hours but wasn't charged. Knaggs, Hadley, Robert Rich, and Koubary were all charged with conspiracy with the intent to import cocaine into the UK.

"I was later moved to a Doncaster prison in the north of England, and my prison category was downgraded to a Category C. But suddenly in August 2010, I was arrested inside the prison and taken into the isolation unit, where I was designated a high-risk Category A prisoner. The police had new evidence against me. I was then transferred to Woodhill Prison to the unit where the most dangerous prisoners were kept, some of whom were serving a life sentence.

"The new evidence that led to me being charged again with a conspiracy to import cocaine into the UK was all the evidence from the Yahoo! emails that I never used and that Rich, Hadley, and Duberly only used. The police said they managed to recover all the deleted emails from Yahoo!, which was not possible, but the court accepted it. For that reason, Knaggs later took Yahoo! to court in the US.

"A few months later, I was taken to a court hearing where I was represented by Daniel Berman Solicitors. A trial date was set, and I was taken back to prison. Upon my return to prison, I had to deal with a problem. A prisoner serving a life sentence began to shout and scream that, at the first chance he got, he was going to murder me, and that nothing would happen to him because he was already serving life.

"I don't know what his problem was, but about a week later, a medical team was called to this prisoner's cell and as soon as they arrived, he managed to steal a pair of scissors from a nurse. He attacked the team and then ran to where I was. I managed to get myself behind a door. The inmate began stabbing himself in the stomach, while swearing furiously at me for about ten minutes until some of the prison guards managed to control him. I was taken back to my cell, which was closed while this crazy man was around.

"Weeks later, my defense solicitor Mr. Daniel Berman produced my defense statement to the court without my consent, At the beginning, I ignored this move, but later, in court, I realized that the defense statement presented by my solicitor wouldn't defend me in any way.

"The trial lasted about five weeks. I was put on trial with my brother, Hector. He was totally innocent of any crime, but the British authorities wanted to involve him in the conspiracy of which I was accused. I told him to go to the witness box, point his finger at me, and accuse me. He was shaken but agreed to do it.

"When His Honor Judge Chambers, Q.C, called me to the witness box, I refused to go because I disapproved of my defense statement. At the end of the trial, the judge asked the jury for their verdict. It found my brother *not guilty*. However, the jury couldn't reach a decision about me. The judge gave the jury more time, but they still couldn't reach a majority decision. So the judge disbanded the jury and set a retrial in six months in October 2012.

"I wrote to Judge Chambers, asking him to change my defense solicitor because of the problem with my defense statement. I hadn't seen it or signed off on it before the trial. A week later, I was called to a court hearing where the judge refused my application, ruling that I had to keep the same defense team. I refused, and Judge Chambers, after a long ruling, withdrew my defense team, ordering me to represent myself in my retrial. I would have no defense solicitor at my trial.

"I wrote to the Crown Prosecution Service, challenging them about the evidence in the case. I asked, since I was now representing myself, how could I possibly build my case from inside a prison? The court ignored my application. I then made another application to the court, asking it to reconsider my situation regarding my legal representation."

Jesus also applied for a McKenzie Friend to help with his defense. In the British legal system, a McKenzie Friend assists a litigant in person by prompting the defendant, taking notes, and quietly giving advice. They needn't be legally trained or have any professional legal qualifications. Although in many cases a McKenzie Friend may be an actual friend, it is often somebody with knowledge of the area and the presumption is heavily in favor of admitting a McKenzie Friend into court.

About a week after applying, Jesus's request for a McKenzie Friend was denied. He was told to be ready for the retrial in October.

"Just before the start of my retrial, I still hadn't received all the legal documents from the Crown Prosecution Service that was being held by my former lawyer, Daniel Berman. Moreover, because I was a high-risk prisoner, I was not allowed to go to the prison library to prepare my defense. I wrote to Judge Chambers requesting that I be given my legal documents. He instructed the Crown Prosecution Service to contact Daniel Berman and get them for me. I finally got them on 10 October 2012. My retrial would start 24 October 2012. I had two weeks to prepare my defense.

"I applied to the court and to Judge Chambers requesting that I change my defense solicitor. A week later, I was called to a court hearing where the judge refused my application and ruled that, once again, I had to keep the same defense team. Again, I refused to do that. Judge Chambers, after a long ruling, withdrew my legal aid. This meant I had no defense solicitor, and I would have to represent myself in my retrial.

"At 10 a.m. on 24 October, the date of the start of my retrial, I was taken to Birmingham Crown Court in the morning and put in a cell. Meanwhile, the court selected the twelve members of the jury without any participation from me, my defense. When I arrived in the court room, I was told by Judge Chambers that the jury had been selected and the retrial would start now. I was ordered to be seated behind a security glass surrounded by more than five police officers.

"I watched the jury enter the room, hoping to see some black or colored members. I thought they would be favorable toward my case. But out of the twelve jurors there were only two from minorities. The rest were all white. I thought to myself: 'I'm going to be found guilty of a conspiracy.'

"The Crown Prosecution Service began presenting their evidence to the jury. A few minutes later, I stood up and asked for a translator because there were a lot of legal terms I didn't understand. The judge ordered the jury out for a break and then told me: 'Mr. Henao, your English is perfect.' He refused to give me a translator for my defense. I told the judge and court that I felt as if I was being bullied and not treated fairly. The court ignored my plea, and the retrial proceeded. I would have to defend myself; not only alone, but without a translator.

"On many occasions during the trial, I interrupted because I didn't understand many of the legal terms being used. I was invited by Judge Chambers to testify, but I declined. Then the judge actually offered me the help of a translator, but I refused. As I told the court, yes, I did need a translator, but now there was no point since my trial was coming to an end.

"Throughout my retrial, the jury didn't hear a single word in my defense. The few times I glanced at the jury, I saw them looking at me with hate. I was convinced they thought I was guilty. It didn't help that each day I was taken to court as a high-risk prisoner accompanied by seven or more prison guards. Even in the court room they sat at my side. This gave the jury the impression that I was a very dangerous man.

"Witnesses were called, but I didn't ask any questions because of the language barrier. About two weeks later, the prosecution finished presenting their evidence. Meanwhile, back in prison, for the next week, I managed to get the help of another inmate, who wrote things out for me that I could read to the jury.

"The only opportunity I had to speak to the jury came on 5 November. I stood up and started to read what the inmate had written for me. But the judge interrupted me and ordered the jury out of the room. After some discussion between the judge and the prosecution, I was told I wouldn't be allowed to present or contradict the prosecution's evidence because I had been offered the opportunity to get into the witness box but had refused. I would only be allowed to explain my participation in the conspiracy.

"The judge asked me if I understood, and I replied: 'Your Honor, I do understand part of it, but I don't understand the legal terms.' The court just ignored me. Then the jury was called back into the court room. I was allowed to read some of the stuff I had written down in my cell. In my own words, I explained to the jury: 'Members of the jury, as all of you can see, the conspiracy I was accused took place in mainland Europe and not the United Kingdom. Let me explain to all of you. Say that you and your friends planned a trip to Paris, but without telling you, your friends also planned to go to London after Paris. You are totally unaware of the trip to London. They made this decision without you, meaning you are part of the plan to travel to mainland Europe but not part of the plan to travel to United Kingdom. I was involved in a conspiracy that took place in Europe, but I never agreed to the part involving the United Kingdom.

"After my presentation, the jury went out for a break. When they returned, the foreman asked the court a question: 'We want to be clear. If the conspiracy did not involve the United Kingdom, does that mean he isn't guilty?'

"Once again, the jury was excused from the court room. The judge and prosecution had a long conversation in open court. The prosecution told Judge Chambers that I was accused of planning the importation of drugs that led to a conspiracy because the plan was already agreed to by the other conspirators. The judge agreed and said he would explain it to the jury.

"After a break, the jury was called back into the court room. The judge told them their question was discussed, and the court had reached an agreement. The judge said: 'Members of the jury, the accused, Mr. Henao, has been indicted for his involvement in a plan to import cocaine. The conspiracy never materialized. Your question is: Can Mr. Henao still be indicted as part of a conspiracy? I can tell you that a drug conspiracy that took place in another country is not a crime here in the United Kingdom under the law. But Mr. Henao was part of a plan that involved importing illegal drugs into the United Kingdom. After those involved in the plan reach agreement it becomes a conspiracy, and it is a crime.'

"The case resumed. On 10 November 10 2012, the jury was sent out to deliberate my fate. The next day they came back and gave their verdict: Guilty. I was sent to a high security prison. In December 2012, I presented my appeal to the Royal Court of Appeal in London."

Jesus and three others were convicted of conspiracy to import cocaine. He received sixteen years. Russell Knaggs, the orchestrator of the ambitious scheme, was given twenty years. Phillip Hadley received eighteen years. Robert Rich was ordered to serve fourteen years. Anthony Perger, who admitted the charge ahead of the trial, was given a five-and-a-half-year sentence.

Knaggs and his men appealed, claiming that evidence against them had been obtained by illegal email monitoring. In an appeal hearing in December 2018, lawyers for the trio questioned how prosecutors got their hands on email messages between the gang members. Yahoo! said the emails it handed over to law enforcement were obtained because of the company's "auto saver" feature. Different versions of draft emails are stored on Yahoo!'s servers and are available for recovery by law enforcement, even if the user deletes their final draft.

In November 2015, Knaggs' legal team filed discovery orders in an attempt to get more information about how the allegedly deleted emails were recovered. Their appeal was dismissed in August 2018 when the judges led by Lady Justice Sharp said there was "no proper basis" for suggesting the emails were illegally obtained.

The men, however, attempted to fight on by asking the court to grant permission to take the case to the Supreme Court. They said the case involved a legal point of such importance that it should be decided by the country's most senior judges. But Lady Justice Sharp dismissed their application in a short ruling, determining that the prosecution's case against them was "overwhelming."

Lady Justice Sharp: "In our view, there is no proper basis for the suggestion that the Yahoo! email evidence adduced at trial was the product of unlawful monitoring or unlawful snapshotting (sic) of any sort. The consistent evidence of the Yahoo! witnesses was that the evidence was not the product of such conduct, and the evidence provides a clear explanation of why that was so."

Ruiz Henao: "The Royal Court of Appeal accepted our appeal based on the inconsistency of the police evidence in how they retrieved the deleted emails from Yahoo!

We thought it simply was not possible. After many court hearings the two main judges were changed, and the new judges made their ruling on our appeal without listening to the experts we called. We lost the appeal and our sentences were upheld.

"I then appealed in the European Court in Strasbourg. It passed the first stage under the International Human Rights Act because I was in a retrial without a translator. However, when the appeal moved on to the next stage where it is reviewed by a single European judge, it was denied. The only thing I could do now was serve my sentence."

ELEVEN

FREEDOM

Jesus concentrated on doing the time while appealing his sentence. He was hopeful that he would win his appeal and get out of prison, but he decided not to worry about it. He kept a low profile and to himself, focusing on self-improvement and taking several courses in psychology, sociology, math, English, and computer science. Jesus also worked on improving his English.

Ruiz Henao: "In August 2017, while serving my sentence, my brother, Francisco Ruiz Henao, became very ill. He had cancer. I was allowed to visit him under prison guard at the UCL hospital in London. In April 2018, he passed away in a hospice. Accompanied by two prison guards, I was allowed to go to his funeral.

"After this, I was transferred to a Category C prison called Highpoint South near Cambridge in Northeast England. In this prison, it was easy to get into trouble with other inmates. I met a few Colombians imprisoned for the same crime as me, conspiracy to distribute and import cocaine. I also met a lot of petty criminals wanting to get involved in the drug business, and they would pester me for advice.

"On one occasion, while I was in the prison gym, I was astonished when two prisoners came up to me and called me by my nickname in the drug business, which not even the police knew: Lucas. It means *money* in Colombian slang and was only known to the major players in the business. In a long conversation with the two inmates, I learned that they were workers for a major distribution network in London, and that their boss had mentioned my nickname to them on a few occasions.

"When my release date came closer, the police took me to a court hearing where the Crown Prosecution Service tried to get a restriction order put on me that would take effect after my release. They wanted me to provide the police with all my bank accounts in the United Kingdom and in any foreign country. I didn't have any bank accounts. The authorities got everything when they busted me.

"I was still representing myself, so I stood up and told His Honor Judge Chambers that I was a Colombian citizen, and that after my release, I wanted to be deported back to my country. The Crown Prosecution Service argued that I was a British citizen and had a British passport. I provided evidence that I never had a British passport. I told the court that I would never change my Colombian citizenship. The judge said he would consider the prosecution's petition and deal with the matter tomorrow.

"The next day, the court hearing opened with a discussion about my British nationality. I again repeated to Judge Chambers that I was a Colombian and that as soon as my sentence was over, I wanted to be deported. The judge took a few minutes and then said: 'Mr. Henao has never received British nationality. He is a Colombian citizen. The court does not have power over Colombian law. Since he plans to leave the United Kingdom, I cannot impose any restrictions on him.' I was relieved and happy that I had at least won one court hearing. The prosecutors and police in attendance just looked at each other. They were not pleased.

"I returned to prison happy, knowing that as soon as I finished my sentence in the United Kingdom, I would have paid my legal debt and would be a free man with no restrictions. But I was not safely home yet. I would have to avoid trouble in prison, and that was not an easy thing to do.

"I was allowed to cook my own food. I loved cooking bacon. The Muslim prisoners didn't like the smell of bacon, but that didn't stop me from cooking it. I always felt that since I respected their culture, they should also respect mine. A few months before my sentence was to end, a Polish Muslim inmate stopped me from using the cookers. I called him aside in a polite way, but he became very aggressive. My prison cell was next to the kitchen, so I invited him to come to my cell and deal with the matter, just the two of us.

"When he showed up at my cell door, I pulled out a handmade knife and said to him: 'If you come in, I'll kill you. I will say that you attacked me, and I had to defend myself.' But he tried to come in, so I attacked him and cut his hand with the knife. He ran away. I just stood by my cell, knife ready, waiting for him to return, but he didn't. So I went back to the kitchen and cooked my food without any problems.

"Later, I saw him in the prison yard. I was very wary of him, but he walked up to me and said that he had learned I am a well-respected man in prison, and because I have many Muslim friends, he would not bother me. I shook his hand and told him that I respected that he didn't alert the prison guards about our altercation. After that, we became friends.

"During this time, Russell Knaggs was transferred to my prison. He was moved into the same wing where I was, and we became neighbors. I thought it could be a police trap, but it was nice to have my old friend with me again. We would talk every day, but never about illegal business because we were suspicious as to why he was transferred to this prison and put in the same wing as me. If it was a police ploy, they didn't get anything new on me. We never talked about the drug trade.

"Weeks later, immigration authorities came to see me with an application that would allow me to stay in the United

Kingdom after my release. I refused to sign it. I told them that I just wanted to be deported back to my own country as soon as I was released. After the immigration visit, I called my wife and told her to contact the Colombian consulate and have them get in touch with the United Kingdom immigration authorities to issue me a travel document. I would need it since my passport was out of date. That took a long time, more than three months. I had to wait to get confirmation from the immigration authorities that they would book my flight as soon as they received my travel documents from the Colombian consulate.

"Every day I tried to get in touch with the British authorities for news about my flight. I was so excited about getting out. In preparation for my release, my wife brought me four suitcases full of clothes and shoes and left them at the prison reception. In early October 2019, I was told I would be a free man, and that my flight was booked on Avianca Airlines for Thursday, 10 October 2019. I would arrive in Bogotá, Colombia, the next day. I told my family to book their tickets on the same flight as me."

On 10 October 2019, Jesus' day of freedom finally arrived. He had survived his time in prison and was released. He said goodbye to his fellow inmates. They were happy for him.

Ruiz Henao: "At 9 a.m., I was taken to the prison reception where all of my property and the four suitcases were handed to me. I signed my release documents. I was no longer a prisoner. I was just a detainee held by British immigration authorities. I stepped outside the prison. It was wonderful. I could smell the fresh air. I was free.

"They took me to the immigration office in Heathrow Airport where I was allowed to shower and get some new clothes from my suitcase. They let me call my family and friends.

"An hour later, I was handcuffed to an immigration officer and brought to the check-in desk. I asked the Avianca employee if I could be seated next to my daughter. The Avianca employee began complaining that it was not possible to be seated where I liked, and that he had regulations to follow. I got very angry and began shouting at him, saying: 'I've been in prison for a very long time, and I want to be seated next to my daughter. I will sit next to her no matter what you say, even if I have to fight the security and get thrown off the plane.'

"The immigration officer nudged me and told me to calm down. Another female employee overheard the commotion and came up to us. She asked me for my daughter's name. I told her, and she then went to the line with the people waiting to check in to my flight and called my daughter's name. I can remember watching my daughter running to the check-in desk.

"A few minutes later, my daughter and I were taken to the plane before the other passengers. I shook the hand of the immigration officer before I got on the plane and thanked him for taking me on my freedom flight. As soon as we entered the plane, we were greeted by the captain, who told me I would be treated like any normal passenger. I wouldn't be allowed to have alcohol, but my daughter and I could sit together with no one else next to or between us. My daughter and I sat down and cried on each other's shoulder.

"After the eleven-hour flight, we arrived at the El Dorado Airport in Bogotá, Colombia, at 4 a.m., where I was met by two police officers. My daughter went and collected our luggage while I was taken by the police officers to a room where they would fingerprint and photograph me. I was put in a waiting room.

"Two hours passed before they called me. After they were through with me, the immigration official said: 'Welcome back to your country. You are a free man.' They showed me the way out. I rushed to where my daughter was. She was beginning to panic, thinking that I was going to be held by the Colombian authorities. When my daughter saw me, she ran to me, and we hugged each other.

"Now I was totally free and able to go around anywhere I liked. We checked in our bags for our flight to the city where I would live. I shouldn't say where it is. Like everyone else, I have enemies. We don't know what could happen in Colombia. When Griselda Blanco, the Black Widow, was deported to Colombia after her prison sentence in the US, it was big news in Colombia. She had a lot of enemies, and it wasn't too long after her return that she was gunned down in the street.

"I had offered to pay for the ticket. I wanted to be totally free. However, the authorities said that it wasn't allowed, and they paid for the ticket.

"My daughter asked me: 'What do you want to eat?' I said: 'I want a nice, big, juicy steak.' We went to a restaurant in the Bogotá airport. I enjoyed a piece of decent beef, a nice steak, for the first time in sixteen years. I used a silver fork and a knife. Real silverware felt so heavy to use. In prison, all I had were plastic knives and forks.

"I like the food more than anything else since I've been released. I can eat anything I want. What a change from prison! Every day was the same thing. I had to eat a lot of pasta. We got only one piece of chicken a week.

"When we arrived at the city where I was to live, a lot of family and friends were waiting to welcome me back home. I went to my sister-in-law's house, and in the afternoon, I travelled with my daughter to a city, and a house my wife owned. When we arrived, we opened a bottle of champagne and celebrated my freedom. That night I slept on a proper double-sized bed, feeling immensely happy. In the next few days, I applied for my new Colombian ID because the one I had was out of date.

"I've had a couple of years of freedom now, and sometimes I still feel like pinching myself. For a long time, it was so hard to accept the fact I was free. I was in a strange environment. All kinds of people were moving around me. I wasn't use to that.

"It was a strange feeling once again to be close to a woman. At the airport, I had watched three women who were standing and talking. I picked up my luggage and stood really close to them. I just wanted to feel the presence of a woman. My wife would visit me in prison, but for a long time, when I was in high security, we were separated by glass. When they took me out of high security, we sat at a table. I wanted to kiss my wife, but a woman prison guard would come over and stop me from doing that. I'd get mad, but there was nothing I could do about it. I told my wife: 'I love you. We belong together. But in here I can't touch you.'

"The prison system does everything possible to stop human contact. I couldn't even give a hug to my son. I saw a man destroy a room, and it took three guards to subdue him, all because he wanted to touch his wife.

"For the first six weeks of freedom, I was jumpy. I'd wake up in the middle of the night and couldn't believe I was free. It has not been easy being out. I'm still adjusting.

"What a change! The world today is incredible. That's especially true for the technology. When I went to prison in 2003, there was no social media, Facebook, Twitter, streaming services or iPhone. I had to go to a phone booth to do business. Now the cell phone is everywhere. It took me a couple of weeks to get comfortable using the cell phone, but its use is amazing. People can call me from anywhere and talk to me. I can even see the people calling me. I'm not on social media. I just use WhatsApp and e-mail. My daughter advised me not to get on Facebook.

"I think the technology has made it worse to be a drug trafficker. You can become too reliant on technology and that will make you more vulnerable to arrest. The police are very good with technology. They can follow you on the phone wherever you are and find out who you are calling. I use text messages, but I am nervous when I do. I wonder who out there can see the messages.

"I am a religious man, so I wonder how God will judge me. There is nothing in the Bible about drug trafficking or anything to indicate that I've committed a sin by being a drug trafficker. The only time you do a sin is when you make somebody do something against their will. For example, if I rob you, that's a sin. I did it against your will.

"God gave us total freedom and our own will. God put drugs on Earth for us to enjoy Yes, people die because of drugs. But it is their choice. I never pushed anyone to take a line of cocaine. People don't really die from cocaine. They die when they mix the cocaine with alcohol or chemicals. Cocaine use alone has not killed anyone, ever.

"In my opinion, marijuana is the same as cocaine. My brother died from marijuana use. He denied that there wasn't anything harmful with using marijuana, but it destroyed his brain. They want to legalize marijuana, but it's a gateway drug to the use of other illegal drugs.

"I'm through with the drug trafficking part of my life. Now I want to lead a straight life and enjoy my family. After my conviction, I felt a lot of hate and animosity toward the police, but all that has dissipated now. I was guilty. My goal was to sell cocaine. Their job was to catch me. They did their job. That's very good for them.

"I can accept that, but what I can't accept is the fact that the police are liars. They lied about everything. They said they saw me doing certain things. They never saw me doing anything. For example, I went into store and bought some shoes for my orphanage. I put the shoes in a couple of bags and placed the bag in the car's trunk. The police were watching me. Later, in court, they said I was putting cocaine in the trunk. That's an absolute lie, but the court believed them. The bags contained shoes for the children in my orphanage.

"Why did they have to lie? The judge said the police had nothing on me delivering cocaine. You could see in the second case how they lied. Would I have gotten out of the drug trade and stayed out if I had survived in court? Yes, I was through with drug trafficking. I would have stayed out completely. I know some traffickers that made their money and got out. I wanted to do the same thing.

"I make no apologies for my criminal career. Let me tell you the truth about how I feel about being a gangster. I came from the jungles of Colombia to become the biggest cocaine dealer in United Kingdom history. I operated in the world's most security conscious city and beat the police for ten years. I must admit I feel good about that. It's incredible when you think about it. I did it by myself. I didn't have anybody telling me what to do.

"The police took me out, but the War on Drugs is still going on. It will never end because as soon as you have demand, there will be somebody to supply the drugs. The authorities can never win the war. The criminals are always one step ahead of the authorities.

"That's the way it was for me until I made a mistake. I would do it the same way I did it, but this time I would stick to my iron rule: Don't let anyone see your face or know who you are. And don't speak in any car, just in open spaces.

"If I didn't sell the drugs, somebody else would. Demand dictates supply. If you have somebody who wants something bad enough, there will always be somebody who will supply it. That's the history of the War on Drugs. They call it a War on Drugs, but that is a ridiculous term. Illicit drugs are a social problem. They aren't a military problem. You cannot change anything with regard to illegal drugs by waging an aggressive war.

"The way to fight drug trafficking is through education. Make people aware of the harm drugs can do. Most people don't have any idea. If you can make people aware of the harm, you will reduce the demand for drugs. If you educate youngsters at an early age, they will never touch drugs. I grew up in a coca-producing country, but I never did cocaine.

"As for me, I've paid the price for my criminal actions. Now I want to move forward. I have a family I want to enjoy. I have a wife who works really hard. She gives me money and takes care of me.

"I do feel sad. I lost sixteen years, the best part of my life, time that I could have spent with my family. In the end, what is the point of having all that money if I lose time? I can never go back to the years I lost in prison. I am sad about that.

"I don't want to let my family down. They saved me, so I will never resort back to my old life. I promised my wife, daughter, and son that I would never put them in the situation they were in for sixteen years. My son was three years old when I went to prison. Now he is a young man, twenty years old, and I lost sixteen years with him.

"When you're in the day-to-day drug game, you don't think about the future. You put it out of your head. Or if you do, you ignore it. If I didn't have my family when I got out, I might have a different view on the world. Many criminals who leave prison don't have the kind of family-support network that I have. That makes them very dangerous.

"I was in prison writing a letter to my daughter. I was telling her how special she was to me. How she was everything to me. A young prisoner came by my cell and saw me writing the letter. He asked me what I was doing, and I told him I was writing a letter to my daughter. He noticed I was writing the letter in English. He asked if he could read it. I gave it to him. He read it and looked at me. I could tell he was moved. He said: 'If someone I loved, my dad or my mom, had sent a letter like this to me, I would never be a criminal. But I have never received a letter like that.'

"I lost all those years with my daughter. I will never get the time back. All the money I made in the drug trade can't buy the time I lost. My family has said to me: 'Don't do it again.' I promised them I will never sell drugs again. I won't lose my family for that. It would be a very stupid decision. It's a promise I intend to keep. I will never let them down again. To die in prison is something I don't want to think about. Sure, there is the money, the excitement, but fuck it all! Drug trafficking will go on and on, but I will not be a part of it.

"I do have one regret though. I never stashed money away. When I was arrested, the authorities got all my money. It was all in three stash houses I owned and my restaurant. The stash houses were given up. When they searched my home, all they found was five thousand pounds. They forced me to give up the £750,000 in my bank account. I had a Swiss bank account and another account in the Cayman Islands, and I used the money from those accounts to pay my debts in Colombia. When I was arrested, I was determined not to owe anyone money. And I made good on that promise.

"In jail, I read stories about me being a billionaire cocaine dealer. That was quite surprising. Did I really make a billion pounds? When you are drug dealing, you are not counting your money. So I really don't know if I made a billion pounds. All I know is that I made a lot of money, and a lot of it didn't go into my pocket. You need to spend a lot of money on expenses. I estimate that of the money I made in the drug trade, probably only about ten percent of it went into my pocket.

"Right now, I want to enjoy life. Colombia is a lot better today than it was thirty years ago when I left for the United Kingdom. The violence has subsided. The country is more secure. The drug traffickers are low profile. They are smarter, but just as active. But I don't think the Colombians are as powerful in the drug trade as they were in my day. I think the Albanians have taken over."

Today, the United Kingdom has the highest cocaine usage in Europe, and is currently consuming more cocaine than ever. It is no coincidence that this is matched by record-breaking levels of coca cultivation in Colombia. However, there is little evidence that Colombians themselves are heavily involved in the distribution or street trade within the United Kingdom—certainly not in the way Jesus and his fellow drug traffickers operated in the early 2000s. Today, their main role is that of producers and exporters.

Pete Walsh: "No one controls the illegal drug market in the United Kingdom today. It is far too large and diffused for any one group, or even a cooperating 'cartel' group, to establish dominance. The impact of the Dark Web on 'street' dealing has been huge and has allowed numerous participants to operate anonymously.

"However, the Albanians have made a significant impact in recent years. This appears to go back just over twenty years, to the period when the Mejia-Munera twins, originally from Cali, formed an alliance with figures in Greek and Albanian organized crime. Their plan was to ship them many tons by sea, with which they would flood the European market. That alliance had barely begun to operate when it was broken up by a huge international law enforcement operation. But ties had been made between the Colombians and the Albanians, and those ties have been strengthened over time.

"The Albanians appear to have done three key things. Firstly, they were prepared to take almost unlimited amounts on credit. Secondly, they were then prepared to crash the price, while maintaining or even upping purity levels; this enabled them to quickly gain market share over more expensive competitors. Thirdly, they didn't simply re-export the cocaine they had imported to indigenous distributors in each country; they were prepared to send their own foot soldiers across Europe to run local distribution networks themselves. This gave them control over more of the sales chain, and again enabled them to sell more cheaply. It carries risk, however, as it is not difficult for domestic police in each state to identify and target Albanians. But Albania is a poor country and they have a ready supply of willing participants."

But whether it is the Colombians, Albanians, or whoever distributes the drugs, somebody will always want to buy and distribute the cocaine.

Ruiz Henao: "It won't be me, though. I have been out of the drug trade, but I am careful about being sucked back in. All I want to do is relax and enjoy my freedom. I don't want to be busy. I want to be involved with my family. I have to make up for lost time."

In November 2020, Jesus' wife, daughter, and son arrived from London for a visit. The Ruiz Henaos were all together again, a family entering a new phase in life.

"We spent time together and traveled around Colombia. The country had changed a lot for the better compared to when I was last in Colombia. In January 2021, my son and daughter had to return to London to continue with their studies and work, but my wife stayed with me. Each night it is nice knowing that I can go to bed whenever I want and wake up at whatever time I want. I've been stopped by police a few times while on the road, and they are always surprised when they check on me and find out who I am and that I haven't been a problem since I came back to Colombia. Why would I be? I've been living a very peaceful life, one full of happiness and freedom."

ACKNOWLEDGEMENTS

We would like to thank all the people who helped make this book possible.

Jesus Ruiz Henao would like to thank his wife Maria Cristina for her courage, love, and dedication to stay by his side and for helping him recall many of his life events.

To his daughter and son for their support, helping him to stay strong, and to keep going and for their incredible words of support and encouragement to write his life story.

And to Mr. Ron Chepesiuk, whom he first met in person in Bogotá, Colombia, and without his help, he could never have written this book. He became my friend, my manager, my writer, and I'm immensely grateful for his passion and dedication to write this book. God bless you, Ron. Love and respect, Jesus Ruiz Henao.

Ron Chepesiuk would like to thank Barbara Casey for selling the project and reading the drafts of the book. Barbara certainly helped make the book better.

Thanks also to his nephew, Ivan Aranda Alvarez, for his continuing support and for reading the manuscript.

To law enforcement officials who patiently sat for interviews and provided background information, including Ian Floyd, Stephen Lear, Ian Munro, and Peter South. These sources also provided background information that was useful.

To Pete Walsh, a renowned expert on Britain's War on Drugs and the author of the classic, *Drug War: The Secret History*. His insightful comments throughout helped make this book better, and I appreciate his support.

To the publisher, WildBlue Press, for taking on the project and shepherding it to its publication.

To Jackie McFadden, for digitizing several the photos used in this book.

And, finally, to Jesus Ruiz Henao for letting Ron tell his remarkable story. The friendship they established along the way has enriched Ron's life.

BIBLIOGRAPHY

Interviews

- Jesus Ruiz Henao

- Peter Walsh

- Ian Floyd

- Stephen Lear

- Ian Munro

- Peter South

Books

- Bean, Philip, *Cocaine and Crack: Supply and Use*. New York, St. Martin's Press. 1993.

- Chepesiuk, Ron. *Narcos Inc.* Maverick House

- Walsh, Pete, *Drug War: The Secret History*. Milo Books. Birmingham, United Kingdom. 2018.

Articles

• "Billion Pound Drug Gang." *Daily Mirror*. 7 January 2006

• "Bus Driver Who Ran Billion Pound Cocaine Racket." *Daily Mirror*. 7 January 2006.

• "Colombian Cocaine Barons, Jailed." *BBC News*. 6 January 2006.

• "Colombians Jailed as UK Drug Ring Smashed." *The Guardian*. 6 January 2006.

• "Conisbrough Dealer Behind Foiled Colombia Drugs Plot Loses." *Rotherham News*. 22 November 2018.

• "Defense Lawyers Claim That Six Months of Deleted E-mails Were Recovered—Which Yahoo's Policies State is not Possible." *Motherboard*. 22 July 2016.

• "Judge Orders Yahoo to Explain How It Recovered 'Deleted' Emails in Drugs Case." *Motherboard*. 22 July 2016.

• "Doncaster Man Dubbed 'UK's Cocaine Mr. Big' Loses Latest." *Doncaster Free Press*. 15 November 2018.

• "Drug Dealer Becomes Northampton Prison's Interior Designer." *Birmingham Mail*. 3 January 2011

• "Drug Smuggler to Remain in Prison Judge." *Barnsley Chronicle*. 10 August 2018.

• "Long Jail Sentences for Cocaine Smuggling Gangsters." *Independent*. 7 January 2006.

• "Men Lose Appeal Over Cocaine Smuggling Plot Convictions." *BBC News*. 15 November 2018.

• "1 Billion Pound Cocaine Cartel." *Daily Mirror*. 7 January 2006.

• "Prisoner Russell Knaggs Guilty of Colombia Cocaine Plot." *BBC News*. 22 February 2012.

• Richard Alleyne. "Refugees Ran a £1bn Network from the Suburbs." *Telegraph*. 7 January 2006.

• Cowan, Rosie. "Smuggling in Suburbia: How Two Men Ran Cartel Flooding UK with 1 Billion Pounds of Cocaine." *Guardian*. 7 December 2006.

• Judd, Terry. "The £1Billion Cocaine Ring: Colombian Dealers Jailed." *Independent*. 7 January 2006.

Primary Documents

• Memorandum. *Regina v Jesus Anibal Ruiz Henao*, Crown Court at Birmingham. 30 April 2012.

• Letter. Jesus Anibal Ruiz Henao to Organized Crime Division, Crown Prosecution Service, Birmingham. 4 July 2012.

• Memorandum. *Regina v Jesus Anibal Ruiz Henao*, Birmingham Crown Court. 5 September 2012.

• Memorandum. Response to Jesus Anibal Ruiz Henao's Application for the Assistance of a McKenzie Friend, Crown Court at Birmingham. 14 September 2012.

• Letter. "Jesus Anibal Ruiz Henao Trial at Birmingham Crown Court," Organized Crime Division, Birmingham. 8 October 2012.

• Letter. "Jesus Anibal Ruiz Henao's Trial at Birmingham Crown Court," Daniel Berman to Sally Perry, Correspondence Department. 12 October 2012.

PHOTOS

Pete Walsh, War on Drugs expert.

Norte Valle cartel leader

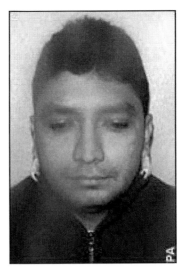

Ruiz Henao's right hand man

Surveillance photo of Jesus Ruiz Henao

£1billion KING OF COCAINE

Mr Big jailed 19 years

THE UK-based boss of a £1 billion global cocaine network has been jailed for 19 years.

Colombian Jesus Ruiz-Henao led a gang that smuggled a ton of the drug – worth £25m – into Britain every year.

But he and more than 30 colleagues were rounded up after a four-year hunt in which more than £3.5m cash and 645kg of cocaine were seized.

Ruiz-Henao, 45, and his deputy Mario Tascon, 32, arrived here in 1990 as asylum seekers. But they set up a "vast and sophisticated operation" with drugs and cash stored at safe houses across London and links to all major UK cities.

One lorry halted by police at Thurrock Service Station, Essex, was stacked with 72 kilos of cocaine.

David Farrell QC, prosecuting, told Southwark Crown Court: "Ruiz-Henao and Tascon played the organisational role in the UK in the repatriation of the proceeds of the organised cocaine distribution here and became involved in

LEADERS: Tascon, left, and Ruiz-Henao

■ **by LAURA NEIL**

substantial cocaine importation and distribution."

Ruiz-Henao, of Hendon, north London, was so crucial to the UK drug trade the cocaine price rose 50% after his arrest in 2003.

Lifted

He said he was responsible for only a small part of what police believe was a £100m-a-year global operation lasting up to 13 years. He was jailed last May

after admitting conspiracy to supply drugs and money laundering, with Tascon getting 17 years.

But restrictions were finally lifted yesterday after the 34th and final member of the gang admitted helping to launder £4m.

Det Chief Supt Sharon Kerr, of the Met's Serious Crime Unit, said: "With 34 criminals now convicted and millions of pounds seized we have effectively wiped out a major gang."

news@dailystar.co.uk

Newspaper clipping announcing conviction

Government document relating to Ruiz Henao

Surveillance photo of Ruiz Henao

Surveillance photo of Ruiz Henao and his crew

Ruiz Henao busted

Ruiz Henao (in middle) in prison

Author (left) with Ruiz Henao in Bogota

Jorge Ochoa, Leader in Medellin Cartel

Orlando Montoya Henao, leader in Medellin Cartel

Carlos Lehder, leader in Medellin Cartel

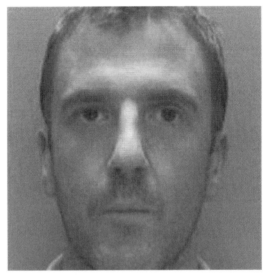

*Gangster whom Ruiz Henao met and
conspired with in prison*

Jeremy Corbyn, British politician whom Ruiz Henao befriended

The poison

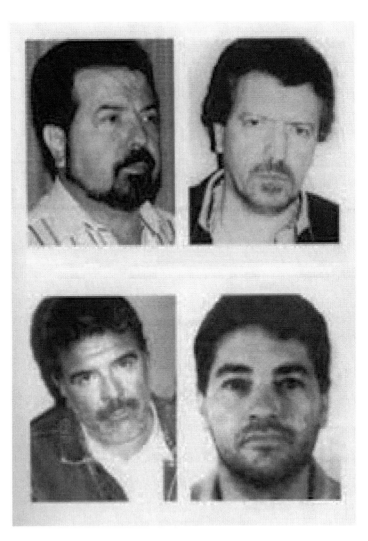

Cali Cartel leaders Top left (Gilberto Rodriguez Orejuela), top right: Miguel Rodriguez Orejuela, bottom left; Jose Santacruz Londono, bottom right: Helmer Pacho Herrera

"Thank you for your interest in our titles. Contact us at **promos@wildbluepress.com** *to learn how to receive a FREE audiobook or ebook of your choice."*

For More News About Ron Chepesiuk and Jesus Ruiz Henao, Signup For Our Newsletter:
http://wbp.bz/newsletter

Word-of-mouth is critical to an author's long-term success. If you appreciated this book please leave a review on the Amazon sales page:
http://wbp.bz/realmrbiga

Index

Y

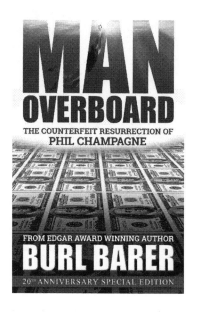

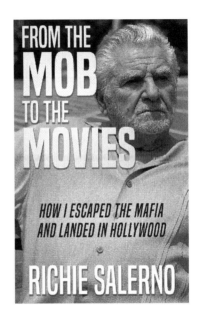

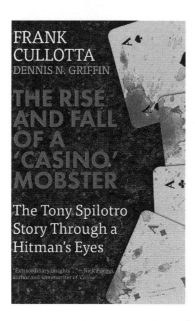

Printed in Great Britain
by Amazon

61881635R00127